W

A TRUE STORY OF LOVE, HOPE, FAITH, DEVOTION AND PEACE

BY RICKIE D. MANESS

Published by Starry Night Publishing.Com

Rochester, New York

Copyright 2014 Rickie D. Maness

This book remains the copyrighted property of the author, and may not be reproduced, copied and distributed for commercial or non-commercial purposes. Thank you for your support.

Rickie D. Maness

When It's Time

Dedicated to the Love of My Life

Karen Elizabeth Miller

Rickie D. Maness

Contents

FOREWORD 7

CHAPTER ONE – ME 9

CHAPTER TWO – HER 15

CHAPTER THREE – HONOR 21

CHAPTER FOUR - THE BEGINNING 27

CHAPTER FIVE - THE MIDDLE 37

CHAPTER SIX - DIRTY LAUNDRY 43

CHAPTER SEVEN - RAY- PART II 51

CHAPTER EIGHT – US 57

CHAPTER NINE - FATE-OR DIVINE INTERVENTION 65

CHAPTER TEN - US, YET AGAIN 75

CHAPTER ELEVEN - A LIFETIME OFFICIALLY BEGUN 85

CHAPTER TWELVE – LOYALTY 93

CHAPTER THIRTEEN - DANCE WITH THE DEVIL 105

CHAPTER FOURTEEN - YOUR REPUTATION PRECEDES YOU 113

CHAPTER FIFTEEN - WHAT NOW? 123

CHAPTER SIXTEEN - "WHEN IT'S TIME" 131

CHAPTER SEVENTEEN – EPILOGUE 145

CHAPTER EIGHTEEN - THE FINAL WORDS 149

Rickie D. Maness

FOREWORD

The Story you are about to read is true. In some cases throughout the pages, names have been changed, not to protect the innocent, but to not give credence to the guilty. This is a story about a woman who captured love in every essence of the word, lived her life to the extent that she gave all she had to those in need, and provided an opportunity for me to be part of her life. This is a story about a person who was so beautiful in life that she could not even realize how much she meant to so many people.

But, I am getting away from the purpose of this story, and getting ahead of myself in trying to explain to the world, what beauty is, from within, and how important it is to give to those that need, to show unequivocal love for all, and to overcome adversities to pursue life.

Karen Elizabeth Miller was a person that inspired hope in all she met, provided a source of comfort to those in need, and did everything in her life to love, give, care, and was the ultimate Advocate for justice in a world, and a system, that has far detracted from that prospect.

There was a time when our Justice System actually cared, and the purpose of Justice was just that, Justice. But it has long gotten away from that, and now it is about numbers, positions, reputations and egos, and as a result, many among us suffer daily. Karen Elizabeth Miller fought every day to correct that, and ultimately the system that she fought so hard to keep intact, turned against her.

I will begin the story by introducing myself, and how I came to be a part of this wonderful woman's life. But, the story is not about me, it is about Karen Elizabeth Miller, and in the end, I hope that those who read this feel an immense desire to do something good for someone else, to honor Justice, and to love everyone, even those accused, and to give a little more of yourselves than you did before.

Some of the incidents that took place in Karen's life have been related to me by Karen herself, by friends and family members and of my personal experiences. Most is written based on memories and not documentation. Do with that information as you will. I did not choose to write this book to fault or place blame on anyone concerning the things that Karen endured in her life. Some things were of her doings by making choices that were not beneficial to a good and healthy life. Others, however, were the doings of people that chose to be mean for the sake of being mean and by some who did not understand the reality of what loyalty to a friend really is. And there are those that, through their own assumptions and beliefs, thought they knew Karen, when the reality of it is, they barely knew her at all, but went about in a manner to inflict dishonesty, untruths and deception toward a woman for their own personal gains.

Karen was a popular figure by most accounts, and loved by those that truly knew her and what she was. But sometimes popularity becomes a threat to others, and Karen was a threat to those that were dishonest and vain, and sought nothing but power and ego satisfaction. So, as you read the story of Karen Elizabeth Miller, realize that, "For there but by the Grace of God go I" and equate it to your own lives as you hopefully garner a better understanding of what life is about and how you can, and should, live each day as if it were your last. But to also live it in a way that lets you leave something good behind.

CHAPTER ONE – ME

I was born in North Carolina, the son of a hard working father, and a mother I never knew from birth. Raised by my grandmother until the age of five, I learned at a very early age to obey the gospel and love the Lord. My grandfather, a Sheriff in the southern county, was a strict person, and although I don't remember much about him, I do know that he was also a caring person. He inspired me to pursue my career in law enforcement that ultimately spanned thirty-four years. My grandmother, the maternal person that raised my brother and me until I was five years old, was a petit woman who taught me how to pray and how to care. At the age of five, my world suddenly came crashing down upon me, without warning, and to a five year old, it was the worst thing that could have happened.

I remember my father coming home from one of his work trips and my grandmother crying, hysterically, and my father explaining, "mama, it's gonna be alright, this is what we have to do." It seems that my father had remarried and brought my "new mother" home with him. We were moving to another state and my grandmother, all 4'10"s of her, was beside herself exclaiming, "You're taking my babies." I remember hiding for quite some time until they eventually found me under my grandmothers fluffy bed, crying. Suffice it to say that, over the next couple of years, we moved around a lot and eventually settled in the Jersey Shore area of New Jersey. That, ultimately, is where I claim my upbringing and where I learned early on how to survive in a word that can be very cruel at times. My "step-mother" became my mother and still is to this day. I learned at the age of ten or so that I had two sisters that had been separated from my brother and I and eventually my father and step-mother had three other children that are my brother and sisters. We never used the word "half" in describing our relationships, and to this day still do not.

Rickie D. Maness

In my high school years I met my "real" mother for the first time, and although a stranger for all intents and purposes, I felt a connection with her. It was not a connection of love or even maternal being, but, in retrospect, just a connection to close a small void in my life that was rarely thought of, but often present. It wasn't until I eventually moved to Florida that I became friends with my "real" mother, and, as life would have it, a short time later she died.

My move to Florida was one of self-preservation. Although street-wise, and fond of my being raised in New Jersey, I knew that if I stayed in the town I grew up in, I would wind up like so many of my friends, in jail, in poverty, or in the grave. I had just gotten out of the Navy and the opportunity arose for me to take a construction job in Florida working for my wife's uncle. Little did I know that my whole life would change, sometimes for the better, and sometimes for the worse, but change nonetheless!

In 1975 I became a Deputy Sheriff for the County Sheriff's Department that I lived in, and over the course of the next 34 years, lived, worked and loved in that town, as both a Sheriff's Deputy and subsequently a Federal Agent, retiring in 2007 from the Department of Homeland Security, the agency newly formed as a result of September 11, 2001. Although those events touched me deeply as I watched the Twin Towers crumble, having seen them often growing up in New Jersey and going to the City regularly, it was a few days after that I realized the personal connection that I had with the events of that day, and one that I shared with Karen Elizabeth Miller, and one that would change my life, yet again, but for the positive.

My sisters, brothers and I were always very close. We fought like rival siblings, we despised each other at times, but we were always there to protect each other, and that we did. In 1979, my older sister killed herself, and it was devastating. I had just been with her the weekend before and was supposed to go over and see her again the night that she shot herself in the little pool tavern she owned in Hollywood, Florida. She was a very complex person, who loved and lived life to the extreme, but in the end, life became too much for her to handle, and ultimately she played the losing card. It was my first run-in with death in this manner, and would not be the last. I spent years asking why? What purpose is garnered? What good can come from this? I still don't have the answers to those questions, even as I struggle with them, yet again.

When It's Time

Shortly after her death I got remarried, having divorced from my high school sweetheart a couple of years earlier, and for the next fifteen years, life took on a role of normalcy. I raised my daughter from my first marriage, enjoyed a fine career and completed my college education. But, over the course of the last 5 years of marriage I realized that "something" was missing. While I truly loved my wife of 18 years, and we enjoyed many good times, it became apparent after the first fifteen years that we were two different people, two people going in opposite directions and two people that had lost their connection, if there ever really was one to begin with. I was raised to always give and take care of those around me. I was raised in a medium income family, at times, the money was short and new clothes were a luxury, but we were never without and never felt that we were. I used to tell people that I never heard my dad say he loved me until the final years of his life, but I also never doubted that he did.

My wife at the time, was raised in an upper-middle class environment, and believed early on that the measure of success was how much you made. Although it wasn't prevalent in her father, a World War II Navy veteran, it sure was prevalent in her brothers and mother, and also in the circle of friends she kept. I remember sitting in a restaurant with her family one night when her younger brother made the comment, "if you don't make at least $200,000 dollars a year, you are nothing." He of course did not make that kind of money, but his goal was to eventually do so, since that would somehow validate his success.

For nearly 15 years I spent every Thanksgiving, and more than a few Christmases, at her older brother's house at whatever city he and his family was living in in Florida. I didn't want to, but as the husband, I was required to. After all, it was "important" to my wife. The pervasive attitude of success through income was all around there as well. Even the children of my then brother-in-law, were adapting that philosophy. The only one that didn't have it was my wife's father, the Navy Veteran. He and I used to go for rides alone and he would confide in me how ridiculous the thoughts of his children were and that none of them knew anything about life in general, and how to struggle in particular. The only time I heard that man use any swear words was when he and I were alone. At his funeral I gave one of the eulogies and cried.

A couple of years later, after almost 20 years together, I was informed by my wife, at two a.m. in the morning, while her mother was in our spare room, that she did not want to be married to me anymore.. After some harsh words, lots of tears, and even some attempts at reconciliation, we divorced in April of 2000. It seems she did not want to waste too much time and informed me that the counseling wasn't working; she had taken half the bank account and rented an apartment for herself. And, oh, "can I borrow your truck to move?" Given the fact that we were merely roommates for the past few years, I wouldn't have guessed the audacity to be any less. To say I was devastated was an understatement. After all, I had stuck through a marriage that had little to do with me for the last few years, and everything to do with her. Although I probably was not a good man at times, I always thought I was a good partner and husband, sticking beside her in the numerous career changes and financial adventures that she invested in over the course of our last 8 years together. I had just had a major surgery as the result of a workplace injury, received a large cash settlement, and paid off her car, bought an IRA for her, purchased stocks for her from the company she worked for at the time, and placed a large amount of money into the savings.

To classify our divorce as contentious would be understating the process. While I tried everything to make it right, she tried everything to make "me" wrong, to the point of actually writing a letter to every member of my family and telling them how cruel I was during our marriage of 18 years. My family was shocked, and knew the truth. I was hurt and thought my life was over. After all, what did I do to deserve this? At one point in time I actually considered ending it all, knowing full well that I would never find love again or at least believing that at the time. The fact that I now had an adult daughter from my previous marriage who depended on me, maybe more than she should have, and still does, would eventually bring me back to reality about taking my own life.

As I reflected back in later years, it wasn't my love that was bruised, it was my ego. I would have stayed in that marriage no matter what, and the fact that someone "didn't want me anymore" was more than my self-esteem could handle.

When It's Time

I don't write this part of the story for any other reason than to explain, and preface, the relationship I had with Karen Elizabeth Miller, my third wife, how it came to be, and the difference true love makes in one's life. In order to know Karen, you have to understand me, and the complete transformation that took place in my person, as a result of my relationship with Karen.

Every story has it's beginning, and the beginning of this one is my previous marriage and how the loss of that marriage and the comfortable life I had grown accustomed to brought me to a place I never thought I could be. My former wife of 18 years was a good person, her family is good people, but, we are often products of our environment and upbringing. And, no matter how we try, it is difficult to escape them. Occasionally I run into her brother and we are cordial. I have not spoken to her in nearly 10 years, of any significance. I saw her in a bar a mutual friend and his band were playing in a few years back. The conversation lasted about 2 minutes, along the lines of "how are you, fine, how are you?" Then I left.

I always prided myself in sticking it out when things were tough and also in knowing, or at the very least believing, that I was a good person. At one point shortly after we were married I did have a period of indiscretion where I thought I was in love with someone else. Most of it was my own doing and I accepted the blame; however, some of it was her doing as well, since the desire to be successful and make money became an obsession to her, at least from my point of view. I quickly became number eleven on her top ten list of things to pay attention to. But even after that, and after contemplating divorce, we stuck it out for another fifteen years. In January, 2000, that all fell apart. We divorced shortly thereafter.

In 1987, after a nearly 10 year stint with the Sheriff's Department, I completed my Bachelor of Arts Degree and was offered a position with the United States Customs Service. As a Sergeant in the Narcotics/Vice Division of the Sheriff's Department, I had occasion to work with Customs Agents now and then but never really knew much about them. I, along with three other members of the Division did attend a 2 day Cross-Designation Training Course in Marco Island, but to be honest, I don't remember much about it, other than we managed to have some pretty interesting Happy Hours in the Hotel where we were staying.

That was in 1985. So, when the opportunity came to "go federal," I hesitantly took the chance. I say hesitantly because, to me, being a Sergeant in the Sheriff's Department was the best job there was. It was fun, we were a brotherhood and I really enjoyed the job. So, as I say, hesitantly I decided to go with U.S. Customs as a Special Agent in the Investigations Division in my home town. I literally moved offices three miles away.

The first two years of my new career encompassed much training including four stints at the Federal Law Enforcement Training Center in Brunswick, Georgia. It was actually quite boring and I often wondered if I had made a mistake. As my career progressed and I advanced, I became more involved in the types of investigations that Customs did, including major smuggling and money laundering investigations. I prided myself on my integrity and ability to complete complex investigations to closure. Many cases involved international crimes and I had the chance to work closely with police agencies from other countries. This is important to the story because, had I not taken the chance that fate offered me, I would have not ventured on the journey that unfolded; the journey that brought me together with the love of my life.

I thought I was a smart and intelligent person that could tackle and handle any issue that life put before me. I thought I knew all about the Justice System and how intricate the parts were that intertwined every day to complete the Due Process that all are provided. I thought I knew how to be a man, a father, a lover, a husband and an all-round good partner. That is, until I met Karen Elizabeth Miller. Our first meeting was one as professionals, but we immediately garnered respect for each other's abilities and intelligence. While she often chided me that she didn't understand "what exactly it is you do," she felt very confident that she could use that to her advantage should the time come, in a professional venue, if she had to. Fortunately, for both of us, that precept was never tested and our relationship fostered as a result of our professional admiration and respect for each other. We became friends instantaneously, that is, until we lost touch with each other for several years.

CHAPTER TWO – HER

Karen Elizabeth Miller liked to tell people she grew up in Philadelphia and was a "Philly" girl. But she was also a Redskins fan, and no self-respecting "Philly" girl could ever root for the Redskins in good conscience. Her grandparents, on her father's side, owned a farm in Pennsylvania and Karen spent many a summer and weekends on that farm. As a young girl she had moved to Washington D.C. with her mother who was employed by a Defense Contractor and, for the most part, that was where Karen grew up. The life in D.C. was exhilarating for Karen and taught her a lot about the continual quest for justice and equality. But the hours spent on the farm in Lancaster, Pennsylvania, those happy hours with her grandparents on her father's side, taught Karen about compassion and living life to the fullest.

Karen learned to drive when she was thirteen years old as her grandfather would let her drive the old pickup around the farm, much to the dissent of her grandmother, who seemed to be the more responsible one of the two when it came to setting boundaries for a teenaged girl. It was not uncommon for her grandmother to return from a trip to the local market or hairdresser to find Karen perched atop the steeple roof of the big red barn while her grandfather casually looked on. Her grandmother would feign anger which would quickly turn into concern then begin scolding both Karen and her grandfather for allowing this child to climb up to the top of the barn where she inevitably was going to "fall and break her neck" someday. Karen never fell, her grandmother never really got angry and grandpa continued to teach Karen about life and about taking chances to elevate yourself as high as you could go. Those lessons never left Karen and became an integral part of who she was and fueled her desire to succeed, not as a lawyer in and of itself, but as a Defender of Justice, one who looked out for the regular people, people the same as her grandparents in Pennsylvania. Karen often reminisced about her grandparents, who were long deceased, and the time spent on the farm. She missed them both deeply but also had an undying gratitude for the happy moments they provided in her childhood, a childhood that had some unhappy times as well.

When Karen was eight years old her father, who was divorced from her mother and lived in New York, suddenly moved from New York, eventually settling on the west coast. To Karen, he might just as well have moved to Australia. The weekends of hopping on the Amtrak from D.C. to New York, being greeted at Grand Central Station by her father, then dancing along the Manhattan streets singing various verses of "Georgia Girl," came to a sudden and crashing end. She never understood, and no one ever tried to explain, how a man could just get up and leave his child and start a new life, with a new wife, in a new city thousands of miles away. The relationship that she had with her father, a very smart man who had multiple degrees from a prestigious business college, was forever fractured, the fact that the situation was never fully addressed by anyone led to the beginning of the feelings of abandonment, and failure, that no young girl should have to endure. Karen, for years to come, would struggle with that concept in her personal life, the concept of how someone, anyone, could just forgo their family and start a new life, a new family, a new beginning. How someone as smart as her father, could leave his only daughter and not look back, and how she was never presented with the real reasons behind the divorce and the move until later on in her adult life.

While Karen did not have a good relationship with her father in her formative years, she tried to maintain the relationship between her children and him later on. Her father had long suffered from an addiction issue which led to the eventual divorce. He had managed to keep it under control and has been "clean and sober" for over 35 years. But to Karen, it was the addictive gene that he passed to her that she resented him the most for, that, and the thought that he never really knew her, didn't take the time to know her after he moved, and never understood that a young daughter needs guidance from both parents, even divorced ones, and that, if you truly love your children, you are always there for them and, without being told, know exactly what they need.

When It's Time

Karen had once told me that the fact that her father, in an attempt to be a good father, bought her a car at the age of sixteen was indicative of how little he knew about her. While most sixteen year old girls would have been elated, the dye had been cast for Karen's misunderstandings, even to the point of resentment at times, about her father. Misunderstandings that carried into her adult life and helped set the stage for problems in her own life. As she stated "…he bought me a "green" car which showed that he had no idea who I was as a person. I hate green." This may seem a bit harsh, and one could say that Karen was the one who wasn't understanding or appreciative, and was being self-centered. But the hurt that she felt by her father's "desertion," as she saw it, was never going to be amended. The perception that he didn't know her fueled the perception that he didn't care or take the time to know her. A "green car" to Karen was just another example of what she missed out on as a child growing up with a single mother and an absentee father.

On the other side of the issue was Karen's mother. It was her mother's side of the family that brought out the desire to succeed and fight for justice. The one fallible part of the equation, however, was that, as a result of living with her mother for most of her life, and the environment that her mother was raised in, she never learned to overcome adversities and to deal with problems. Many good things came out of her relationship with her mother, and she absolutely adored her mother, often telling me what a great time she had growing up in various cities and how her mom was always there, a fact that was exemplified in Karen's mind by her father "not being there." The one thing missing was the ability to learn how to deal with problems as they arose. According to Karen, her mother was raised in an environment where bad things didn't get resolved; they got ignored, buried or relocated. Karen often repeated to me the family philosophy on her mother's side, "we don't talk about bad things; we ignore them and then move." A prime example was her constant relaying of the adage, "there are two rules, Grandma doesn't have a drinking problem, and we don't talk about Grandma's drinking problem."

While her Grandmothers of course did not have a drinking problem, it was just an example of how Karen seemingly was taught about dealing with issues and problems, and how she utilized this philosophy in her own life as she was confronted with issues over the course of the next 30 years. Perception can be reality when you use it to overcome, or in some case, not overcome, those issues that need to be addressed.

As a young girl, Karen was moved a lot, and even as an adult, she often found herself running from problems, never fully comprehending that they do follow and eventually surpass. But Karen's running and relocating, never detracted from her love for people, her love for her mother and children and especially for her love of those in need.

While the issues surrounding Karen's inability to address setbacks, hurt and emotional upheaval was cast, for the most part, on the maternal side, Karen's penchant for justice was formulated on her mother's side of the family as well. Her grandfather, her mother's father, was a career General. He had survived the landing at D-Day and was a stoic example of honor, integrity and pride. He was a man who tolerated very little insubordination from the men and women under his command, as well as from his family. But he was also a man that had witnessed the spoils of war, and appreciated life. While the General taught her about loyalty and respect, it was her grandmother, her mother's mother, who taught her about the importance of graciousness and social being. Karen was as comfortable on the streets of D.C. or "Philly," as she was at a cocktail reception at the home of one of her grandfather's West Point classmates. When Karen decided to go to law school, she returned to Washington D.C. While at law school, Karen had a short internship at a U.S. Congressman's office. There she learned about the workings of the political machine. Although not one to be interested much in politics, she developed an understanding of the necessity for litigation and compromise in order to achieve a favorable outcome. But the fight for justice that was inherent in Karen's make up was developed as a result of her heritage on her mother's side.

When It's Time

Karen had an ancestry that dated back to Colonial existence. Not one to classify herself as a Red, White and Blue Patriot, she did have a great respect for what her ancestors endured by taking a stand for Liberty and Justice, knowing that the majority of the original Patriots, those that put their lives on the line to go against the King of England and help formulate a new country, died penniless, impoverished or imprisoned. She always felt a strong urge to fight for the Rights of the people. The Constitution, to Karen Elizabeth Miller, was not just a paper signed long ago, it was an edict on Freedom and Liberty and the preservation of Justice. The Bill of Rights was the basis for equality and the thing that drove Karen to be the best defender she could be of the Rights of people and the protection of "Justice for All!" Karen Elizabeth Miller was a true fighter in the war against injustice, and she never met a case she didn't want to go full bore with.

Eventually this penchant would also catch up to her, as both Karen and I saw over our years together in the professions we were in, that it truly isn't about justice, it's about so much more, and it, at times, can be cruel and vicious and devour those that are not strong enough or passionate enough to endure the fight. There are those that enter into the system as prosecutors, defense attorneys, and even police officers that have a true calling. And, just as well, there are those that enter into the system because of a need for power, celebrity status, ego satisfaction and political gains. There is very little that separates the two, and it is only those with the true understanding of what this country was founded on and necessity for "Justice under the law" that are the true protectors of our Rights, Liberties and Pursuit of Happiness. The system itself can be pervasive, and often times breeds character flaws that hinder its success. But, for the likes and devotion of individuals such as Karen Elizabeth Miller, the system would collapse upon itself, drawn slowly down by its own corrupt nature, to the extent that even anarchy would be a welcome relief. Understanding that I gave my entire life to this profession and tried to always maintain my integrity and compassion for the edict that "even good people make mistakes," I have also seen the underbelly of what the system can be. But it wasn't until I met Karen that my eyes were truly opened.

Karen attended college in her senior year of high-school. She excelled as a student at the University of Miami, and put herself through Law School at American University, Washington School of law, in Washington, D.C. She moved back to Miami upon graduating and passed the Florida Bar on the first go. She often bragged that she was "high" when she took the exam, but I think that was just what she liked to say. She began her career in the Public Defender's Office in Miami, Florida. Karen was "Mensa" smart; but she never used it to build herself up, or to put anyone else down. Her ability to talk to the brightest on their level, and the not so bright on theirs, was a unique characteristic that was formulated in her upbringing. The beginning of her career in Miami, was, unbeknownst to her, the beginning of the end of her happiness for some time to come. Her desire to be on the "right" side of the fight for justice led her into personal situations that she could have never foreseen had she been able to understand that some people are just evil, and others have their own agenda, and that agenda may be at a price that somebody else has to pay. Karen looked for and felt the good in people, not the bad. And she always gave everyone the benefit of the doubt. Unfortunately, that benefit would lead to a life of abuse, heartbreak and emotional distress that, in the end, would become catastrophic.

CHAPTER THREE – HONOR

"Injustice anywhere, is a threat to Justice everywhere." That slogan by Dr. Martin Luther King Jr. was pasted on the wall of Karen's Office, and she even had coffee mugs made up containing the same. Karen truly believed the words of Dr. King, and she truly believed that, as her ancestors, she was placed on this earth to right the wrongs of those accused, and to offer everyone the chance at Justice. That is why Karen became an Assistant Public Defender in the first place. She knew that the most critical injustices were given on the backs of those that could least afford to defend themselves. And, in order to fight the true battle, it had to be fought in the trenches, and in the trenches she stayed for the better part of her adult life and career. Those trenches also had their price. The people that could most afford to pay for their justice, as well as the ones who were self-appointed to dole out justice, were also the ones that delivered the least amount of justice as a whole. Karen took on the role of public defender with a passion that few in her profession had seen, or could match. In addition to being passionate, Karen was also a brilliant litigator and knew the laws and the judicial aspects better than anyone, and that knowledge and passion was eloquently bestowed upon her in gratitude by the Florida Third District Court of Appeal in an Appellate Decision in December, 1991.

The case, which is public record, was "Edward Hightower v. The State of Florida, No. 91-488, December 10, 1991."

The facts of the case are not as important as the Decision of The Court and the written opinion of the Justice in overturning the Conviction. The Prosecutor, during the trial, used the tactic to attack the "credibility of the defense counsel," that being Karen Elizabeth Miller. Karen, realizing that this tactic was an improper use of the Due Process provision contained in the Constitution of the United States, also realized that it was an outright attempt to sway the jury by presenting the defense counsel, and Public Defenders specifically, and the defendant, in a negative light for the simple purpose of obtaining a conviction, regardless of Due Process.

A portion of the decision by the Appellate Court in overturning the conviction states: "…the prosecutor's comment implied to the jury that defense counsel was only representing the defendant because she had no choice and was forced to." The comments made by the Prosecutor at closing arguments to the jury were; "Now, Ms. Miller is an excellent attorney. She's appointed to represent Edward Hightower. She's the Assistant Public Defender. She doesn't choose her clients and it's her job and she does a good one to confuse witnesses, to try and put words in witnesses' mouths as she did on her cross examination." The Court further wrote in its opinion overturning the conviction: "…this improper attack upon the credibility of defense counsel deprived the defendant of a fair trial, thus constituting fundamental error and warranting reversal."

There are many other points made in this particular opinion that show the brilliance of Karen Elizabeth Miller in regards to the law and justice. However, the reason I have written about this here are the comments made by the Justice who rendered the decision on behalf of The Court. Those comments are a true reflection of Karen Elizabeth Miller as a person and as a Public Defender, and gives credence to every Public Defender in the United States. Karen was so very proud of this decision and the comments, as she felt it validated her as a person, a Defender of Justice and as one who was a "true believer" in fighting the fight. Here are the written words of the Appellate opinion as written in the brief:

"There was no reason for the prosecutor to draw the jury's attention to the fact that appellant was being represented by a public defender. There was no reason for the prosecutor to attack the credibility of the public defender. There was no reason to make such outrageous comments about the public defender.

The necessary implications flowing from the prosecutor's comments are that public defenders are second rate attorneys who are forced to represent the guilty, and whose job is to confuse the jury. The ultimate inference is that public defenders are unreliable and untrustworthy, and that they rely on obfuscating the evidence to obtain the acquittal of a guilty defendant.

When It's Time

It is ironic that the prosecutor made such a statement. The public defender epitomizes why so many have entered law school. They seek not fame or fortune. Instead, they seek the higher level of professional satisfaction of representing the people who most need legal representation.

Public defenders stand alone, armed with their wits, training and dedication. Inspired by their clients' hope, faith, and trust, they are the warriors and Valkyries of those desperately in need of a champion. Public defenders, by protecting the downtrodden and the poor, shield against infringement of our protections, and in reality, protect us all."

These written words epitomized Karen Elizabeth Miller, and while Karen rarely brought this decision to the attention of colleagues and adversaries, she always carried it in her heart as a badge of honor, and those that knew her best were well aware of what she had provided to them all as a result of this Court decision.

In the coming years of my relationship with Karen I would witness firsthand her abilities as an attorney and her intelligence as a purveyor of Justice. More than that, I would experience firsthand her compassion for everyone that crossed her path or came into her office needing someone to help them. I watched her take on cases that were far below her capabilities and credibility, simply because an injustice was being done. More times than not, she would handle these types of cases without fanfare and often without charging the client. I observed her giving her last twenty dollars to a client that had just gotten out of jail and had no money for a bus home or food to eat. I watched her every Christmas saunter off to the mall or her favorite store, Target, to buy carts full of clothes and shoes for children of clients that had very little. I was with her as she visited sick colleagues in hospitals, took one of her favorite Judges who had retired and had a major stroke to lunch because few in the profession would visit him or could be bothered by giving some time to a man that displayed honor on the Bench. I drove her to the hospital to be in the delivery room of a client who was having a mid-wife do the procedure because she had no insurance. The child was subsequently named after Karen. Later on, I would go with her to pick up the child from day-care for the day because the mother had fallen back into her habits and abandoned the baby and the father who worked all the time.

Karen felt that the child needed to be given love and affection by people other than day-care workers, and after buying a stroller and toys, would take the child for the day and spend hours with her until the father came by after work to pick his daughter up.

Even when Karen was going through her own hardships and had been beaten down by the system she so eloquently defended, she would drop everything at the blink of an eye if someone was in need, including family members, regardless of the time of day or night. When a local investigator for the prosecutor's office was arrested after an accident that left one person dead, Karen went to the jail at midnight to visit him, because, as she said, "I know what it is like to be all alone there, and I know what it means to know someone cares." She did not go there to solicit business; in fact, it was not her forte and she would not have entertained the idea. She went there because, even though he was on "the other side" so to speak, he was still a human being, and he was in need of a friend. Although they had a casual, professional acquaintance prior to this incident, they became friends immediately afterwards and she stuck by that friendship.

Karen was a genuine Child of God, although her relationship with God sometimes became an issue between us. She always believed that God was the ultimate advocator for Justice and that He was true in His Judgment. She believed that God judges people on their hearts, their deeds and their intentions more than on their Faith. In that regards, she eventually convinced even me that this may just be the case. Karen loved going to church with her family because as she said, "it gives me time to read." She developed a pure relationship with our Pastor and would often call upon him to "give a special prayer" for a client in an upcoming trial. Many times the Pastor would accommodate her request and put a little something in his sermon that only she and I could relate to in response to her request. She would hear his words, smile, give me an elbow to the side and say, "hey, we got this one." She had the "Church Ladies" from the Black neighborhood that adored her praying for her clients, not in an effort to get them off of charges, but a request for Justice and strength to do her job.

When It's Time

Someone once asked Karen how she could "defend people that she knows are guilty." Her reply was always, "defending the guilty ones is easy, you only seek justice and a fair trial. It's defending the innocent ones that are hard." As I grew to love her more and more, I also grew to understand Karen Elizabeth Miller, the person, a mother, a wife, a friend and the compassionate giver, not just Karen Elizabeth Miller the outstanding attorney and exemplary representative of humanity.

Rickie D. Maness

CHAPTER FOUR - THE BEGINNING

Most stories start the beginning with the first chapter. While I have tried to set the stage for knowing the person of Karen Elizabeth Miller and how I came to know her as well through the first three chapters, this chapter is labeled THE BEGINNING because it is the beginning of a life of putting your love and trust into the hands of people who violated both at every turn. A life of having Hopes and Faith in those you surrounded yourself with, both personally and professionally, shattered routinely, and the inability of a person with the love and warmth of Karen to overcome, or even understand at times, that some people are just mean. While Karen Elizabeth Miller was the product of a decent and loving background, she was often times susceptible to the misgivings of that background in believing that everyone was as good and as caring as she. As I relay the events to follow, I relay them through what Karen herself told me over the years and what I learned from friends, associates and family members that all verified, in one way or the other, that these things did happen.

Karen moved to Miami in the early 1980s to attend the University of Miami. She resided with her boyfriend of several years; a man that she always thought was going to be the one for her. A good person, Joe was kind, fun and had two young children that Karen adored and helped raise during the times they spent with their father. Weekends consisted of camping trips, fishing on a lake all day or just "hanging" out at the apartment. Joe was a hard worker, but not one to be characterized as overzealous when it came to making a living. Karen would attend her classes during the day and work intermittent part-time jobs as a waitress or barmaid to help bring income to the home. Their relationship began to deteriorate as Karen progressed in her educational aspirations and Joe remained stagnant in his ambitions to elevate his own future. The reality of the demise of her relationship with this man was characterized to me one day when Karen told me she realized that Joe was never going to go any further than where he was.

Although she truly loved Joe, "...once, when I got really angry at him because he just didn't want to do anything with his life, I threw a book at him, breaking the window behind where he was sitting. He simply got up, and started to walk away, not even wanting to have a discussion or confrontation with me. I asked him where the fuck he was going and he said….."I'm going to get something to fix the window." I knew then that we were pretty much two different people and we split up shortly after that."

Between her split with Joe and attending classes at the university, Karen took on summer jobs as a Hostess on Private Yachts. Her travels on these Yachts took her to the Caribbean Islands and other exotic beach locations. She would often talk about how much fun she had and how much she loved the water, beaches and boats. When she would talk about this experience, and look at some of the pictures she had, there was always a glow and a smile. She was destined, so it seemed, to always live by the water, and it was there that she always seemed the most happy.

After completing her undergraduate studies, Karen applied and was accepted at American University, Washington School of Law, in Washington D.C. It wasn't an immediate transfer from the University of Miami. At one point she attempted to reestablish her relationship with her father. She moved to Seattle and attended classes at the University of Puget Sound for a short time. The effort to rekindle a father-daughter relationship was difficult at best, aided by the fact that she was "in Seattle for God's sake, there's no beaches," as well as the absence from her mother who had always been there for her. Karen missed the big city life, the East-Coast atmosphere and the desire to return to the place she was most familiar with. Karen returned to Washington D.C. and graduated from Law School in 1986. She wanted to return to Miami, as she loved the beach, and she wanted to work for the Public Defender's Office. She did both when she passed the Florida Bar Exam on the first try and was immediately hired by the Public Defender as a misdemeanor trial attorney.

When It's Time

Karen had a small apartment near the water and became best friends with a young prosecutor who was sworn into the Bar with her on the same day. They were assigned the same trial tract as young attorneys in the Misdemeanor Division and would often go to court in the morning for a Docket Sounding, Status Conference or Trial Call, then quickly run out of the building, carrying their bathing suits in their bags, and spend an hour or two laying on South Beach before having to go back to court for the afternoon business. The friendship she developed with this Prosecutor was one that carried on for many years, even though the coming events would locate them miles apart and, at one point, in different states. Karen loved her life in Miami, excelled as a trial attorney in the Public Defender's Office and had a best friend she could totally relate to and confide in. Then she met William.

William was a young strapping Metro-Dade Police Officer of Cuban descent that captivated Karen from the beginning. Recently divorced with two children, William and Karen quickly became friends, as Karen always had a respect for the police and the job that they did, but, only those that had integrity and honesty. Karen would go on "ride-alongs" with William who eventually became a detective, and they became involved romantically. They shared an apartment together, and although, as Karen would often put it, "I never really trusted him because he was such a flirt and a ladies man, but he always made my heart flutter anytime I would see him walk into my courtroom." She became a friend to his children and enjoyed the weekends with them. They made plans to be married, even picked out the place they were going to be married at, and began, Karen felt, building a future together. Although she never really talked about it in detail, the only thing she would say about her time with William was," it was fun, I really loved him, until the day I came home and found that he had taken all of his things and left." The rest of the story was never fully relayed, it was a very painful and devastating time to Karen, and, the fact that William eventually married the woman he left her for was bad enough, but he married her in the place that Karen and he were planning to be married.

While she buried the pain and emotions of that relationship and the events that transpired, she never really got over it, and it was many years before she ever talked to him again. However, as it would turn out, she didn't quite bury it deep enough, and knew that it was the first step to pointing her to a life filled with even more hurt, pain, abuse and torment. That was when she met Ray.

The details surrounding her relationship with Ray are sketchy at best, for over the later years it was a part of her life that she wanted to forget, but unfortunately, prevailed in her emotional caldron, sometimes to the point of pure distress. Karen would often talk about this time, not for the fond memories, but for the ever present nightmares, but never in exact detail. The story takes a turn here, for, as close as Karen and I became, there were still secrets about her relationship with Ray that she chose, or perhaps vainly tried, to hide from everyone. But the devil is in the details, as few as they are, and permeated every aspect of Karen from that point on.

After her split with William, Karen eventually bought a small condo on South Beach, had her favorite car, a small BMW convertible, and had her favorite job going well as her career accelerated. Although emotionally confused and hurt, she tried to put on the proverbial smile every day and act like she was over it. Inside, however, she was distraught, lonely and very vulnerable. She dated, for a short time only, a coworker at the Public Defender's Office, an attorney whose ego eventually got the best of her, and it quickly ended. They remained friends for many years after, although to her, it was a casual friendship as she considered him to be one of the best attorneys she had ever met, and one who taught her much about being a great defense litigator. But he was also a person that, for the most part, was not to be trusted outside of the professional arena. Years later they would reunite as co-workers in a different office and, although she still considered him a great attorney, didn't have much of a relationship with him outside of the office.

Being vulnerable and lonely is one of the hardest things for any human to endure. Decisions that are made through vulnerability, and in an attempt to overcome loneliness, are not usually made with the right frame of mind, and don't often lead you down the right path to happiness. But, in too many cases, they are made anyway and in some instances they work out, and in others, they end badly.

When It's Time

Ray was the one person that Karen should have never gotten involved with. At first he was charming, said all the right things and made her feel good. Although not extremely well educated, he was very smart and made a lot of money in a successful construction business. He quickly swept her off her feet, or, as it turned out, swooped in for the kill. The subtleties of control and abuse are small, and women who enter into such relationships are usually the last ones to realize what they are involved in. Although Karen was a brilliant person and a great attorney, with "street-smarts," she was no match for the cunningness and deception that Ray would perpetrate on her over the next few years. Her emotional vulnerabilities and quest for happiness would also add to her weakness. Perhaps it was her vulnerable state, or the desire, no, more of a dream, and necessity, to have a relationship that led her to the white picket fence in suburbia with a couple of children and flowers on the table, that kept her involved with Ray. Her friend, the prosecutor, had many a run-in with both Ray and Karen about the relationship, as she could see the changes slowly evolving in Karen, and realized that Ray had one agenda, and that agenda was complete control. Eventually, Karen's friends were made distant by her involvement with Ray, and her mother, the one person she always turned to for support and love, was the one person she was not allowed to be with.

Karen and Ray married and had a son. While she was pregnant with her son, Ray forced her to move to St. Louis to live with his mother at first, then their own place. Ray made her sell the condo on South Beach, sell the BMW, and exhausted all of her savings, all the while, keeping Karen secluded from the life she had known, the profession she adored and the friends she had, including her own mother. Karen, at first, followed willingly. Ray was a charmer, but the deeper she got into the marriage and with a son on the way, the more unable she was to break the bonds that Ray placed on her. At first it was just controlling her behavior. Then it became controlling and physical abuse. As Karen would often tell me, "you don't realize it's happening until it's too late, then, you are so beaten down and made to believe that you are nothing, you simply give up and try to exist, hoping that somehow, someday, things will change."

It was not uncommon for Karen to attend family functions and holiday events at Ray's family venues with a black eye, swollen lip or some other evidence of a beating the night or day before. While she was afraid to bring up the source of the injuries, which would always lead to another beating, the one thing that made Karen hurt the most is how Ray's family, even his sister that she had a good relationship with and was close to, never mentioned anything about her injuries or confronted Ray about the abuse that they all had to have known was being done. It was like, in this existence, Karen was invisible, as were the obvious scars, and she could never understand how Ray's family could turn such a blind eye from what was the obvious. As the external wounds healed over time, the internal wounds mounted, to the point where they became a heavy burden on Karen and allowed her to beat herself down, emotionally.

Ray was a strapping man, and injected fear and control into the marriage. Karen quickly learned that it was easier to take the beating than to fight it, and she knew she was trapped in a life that she never imagined, nor ever deserved. Her son was the most important part of her life, and she needed to protect him at all costs, even if it meant existing in the "hell," as she would describe it, that was the life with Ray. When Karen realized that not only was she being subjected to the abuse, but the day she saw her son hiding in the corner, afraid to say anything, was the day she knew, at whatever the cost, she had to protect her son. When the opportunity came for her to make her escape, after nearly three years of torture, she packed her young son into her car, and drove for two days to her mother's condo in Southwest Florida. While still lonely and vulnerable, at least she was free from the man that she came to despise the most.

Karen had a multitude of friends in the legal profession in Florida, and she knew she would be protected if at any time Ray tried to come after her, and he did, repeatedly, over the course of the next two years. Karen renewed her Bar license and got court appointed clients to sustain a moderate income. Karen had a lot of friends in the area, including a host of lawyers and things, at last, started looking up for Karen, and she moved into her own apartment with her son.

When It's Time

Karen spent the next year trying to piece back her life and regain her emotional confidence, to the point of where she no longer felt like she was a "piece of shit" as Ray would often tell her. It was also the time when Karen began to drink more and more to forget her loneliness and what she had just endured. Then, the worst possible scenario happened, one that not even Karen could have anticipated, and one that would slowly drag her back into the depths of despair. Ray found her.

Over the course of the next two years, Ray injected himself back into Karen's life, slowly at first, then more and more in an attempt to convince her he had changed. Karen, believing that perhaps he had, felt it was also important to allow her son to know his father and maybe be able to have a solid relationship with a man that at one time appeared as a monster to them both. He eventually homesteaded in Karen's apartment and began to take control again. Karen soon began to realize that the situation was getting out of her control and called the police to have Ray removed. When the police came, she explained that it was her apartment, and Ray, her ex-husband had come over from Miami to see their son, as he often did, but refused to leave. She didn't bore them with the details of his abuse or that she was a constant victim, she just wanted him gone. As she was standing outside the apartment with the police, Ray asked the officers if he could go back inside and get his things then he would leave. They agreed to let him go in and Karen, knowing Ray, pleaded with the officers to not let him go in alone. They let him anyway, against her wishes, and Ray emerged a few minutes later with his personal effects and they escorted him to the parking lot. When Karen went back inside the apartment, she knew immediately that something was wrong. Ray, it seemed, had gone into the kitchen, retrieved a bottle of Clorox Bleach, and then took it into Karen's closet and threw it over every one of her business suits and dresses that were hanging there. Ray had found another way to perpetrate his vengeance and control over Karen, even as he was leaving.

After the Clorox incident, Ray came to visit their son again. Several months had passed and Ray, being the ultimate "I'm sorry" guy, and Karen, being the perpetual believer that people are good, allowed Ray to visit often and spend time with her and their son.

Things went pretty well for many of the visits, then, one night, as Ray again began trying to control Karen and push her back into the emotional abyss, he also threatened to take their son back to Miami with him and not let Karen have him or ever see him again. Karen, emotionally distraught and angry, told Ray, "If I had a gun, I would shoot you." She then called the police to come and help her, but she made the mistake of calling the non-emergency line. Ray, being the master of manipulation he was, called the 911 line and said his ex-wife had threatened to shoot him and he needed help. The police arrived, a female and a male, and approached Ray as the victim. Even though no gun was displayed, nor was one ever possessed by Karen, the police took their son from Karen's arms, gave him to Ray, and arrested Karen for Domestic violence. It seemed that Ray, being the perceptive charmer he was, had convinced the female officer that Karen was a danger and was going to harm him and their son. Karen was astonished, and outraged, at the events unfolding, but was helpless to do anything at that time.

Ray left with their son, and Karen left in the police cruiser. It took eighteen months and over fifteen-thousand dollars in legal fees for Karen to get her son back and had a permanent restraining order issued against Ray. Even having friends in the legal system does not advance the wheels of justice that turn slowly. Karen began to put her life, and her career back together, again, reestablished her reputation as a brilliant defense attorney, and seemed on her way to making her life successful in spite of the things that had befallen her over the last five years. She rekindled her friendship with her best friend, the prosecutor, and began to reestablish her connection with her mother, even buying a house down the street from her mother's condo and was starting to feel "good" about herself. She went into private practice with a friend of hers and had casual relationships here and there. She enjoyed her house and enjoyed living in it with her son but was not really "happy" as she still struggled emotionally from the deceits, lies and abuse that had been fostered upon her by the men in her life up to this point.

When It's Time

She made plans to just go along for a while and be with her son and mother, who lived part-time in the area, and enjoy her friends. She wasn't looking for a relationship and was content being who, and what, she was. But as is often the case, when life seems to be going along the way we plan, it will always deal you a setback, for whatever reason. That's when Karen met the doctor.

Rickie D. Maness

CHAPTER FIVE - THE MIDDLE

Karen was somewhat content, but even contentment for a person who is lonely can be an obstacle when it comes to managing a life that had been filled with emotional hurt and pain. She often found herself wondering why she had been placed in the situations she had and "why" she could not find a person who was kind, generous to her son, and truly cared about her as a person and a woman who exhibited compassion. It seems that when you least expect to find love, be it true love or just a stopover, it finds you, and when you quit searching for it, you find it. Love found her in the strangest of situations, and again cast her into a decision that eventually would affect her emotional stability in ways she had never imagined.

Karen had often thought about having another child, a daughter, one that was the image of her and would be the much needed sibling for her son. She researched the percentages of having a female child by doing certain things at certain times during the course the natural cycle that a woman experiences. She was now over thirty and knew the biological clock would eventually make its last tick and the chances of actually manipulating gender would become more and more difficult. She tried getting pregnant by invitro using anonymous donors from a well-recognized and reputable sperm bank. The one time she thought she was pregnant ended in an early miscarriage. The other times went by without successful results.

During the course of the procedures she often visited Maurice, the OBGYN that handled the procedures and helped her through the emotional distress of them being unsuccessful. Maurice was a slight-built Jewish Doctor who Karen immediately had a connection with. The connection grew as their relationship of Doctor-Patient expanded, and eventually, without planning on the part of either one, they became romantically involved. To say Karen was in love with Maurice would be a stretch. She admired him as a professional, and he was kind and giving to both her and her son. She loved him as a person, but loving someone is far different than being in love with someone.

Karen knew the difference, but she also knew that she had endured a life of deceit and dishonesty from the previous men she had been involved with, and Maurice was anything but that. He offered her a stable environment and treated her with respect and kindness. He would indeed be a good person to raise her son with, she believed, and he subsequently moved into Karen's house. The dream of suburbia was maybe, just maybe, not out of reach after all.

She allowed her son to continue a relationship with Ray, and even after all that Ray had put her through, she still felt the connection to him as the father of her child and a person, who when he wanted to be, was caring and supportive. Ray had long since departed the picture as a permanent fixture, which allowed her to have a "decent" relationship with him and things seemed like they were all working out for her and Maurice.

Maurice and Karen endured some hard times in the local area as a result of their romance. Maurice had been married at the time and moved in with Karen before his divorce. Maurice was well known and well respected in the community and in the medical profession, and Karen had just started to reconnect with her legal profession in a manner that allowed her to regain her pride and confidence. This alone gave them both the stability to endure the inevitable back stabbing and whispers in the dark about them from colleagues and not so good friends. They pretty much did everything together including numerous trips to antique fairs across the state. Maurice was a fanatic for old stuff and even bought an old Volkswagen Beatle for Karen. But Maurice also had a slightly dark side, one that Karen didn't care for but one that she tolerated. Maurice was not an extremely honest man and, given the opportunity to "pilfer" an antique or some other small object, he took great liberties in doing so. This often times infuriated Karen as to her, taking anything that didn't belong to you, was just wrong. The two things Karen despised the most were a person who would steal and a person who would vandalize something just for the sake of doing it. It wasn't like neither Karen nor Maurice could afford the things that he "took," to Maurice, it seemed more like a game, and besides, as he would often say, "they overcharged me on the other things I did buy anyway."

When It's Time

Sometimes in the scheme of things you have to weigh the good against the bad, and as a person, Maurice was good, as a partner, he was very good, and as a caring man, he was great. So, going against the grain of what Karen felt about Maurice's actions, she figured, "if that's the worst there is, it isn't that bad, and eventually, I will be able to convince him to not do it anymore." Karen believed that her time for happiness, and expanding the family with a daughter, was running out so she tolerated Maurice and his idiosyncrasies. But as Karen would soon find out, that was not "the worst there was."

Karen had struggled from the time she was in her late teens with getting involved with the wrong people. These involvements also led to getting involved in alcohol and drug use to the extent of abuse. It seemed that whatever relationship she was in, or whomever she was associated with, the evil head of the demon would always rise in the form of drinking and drugs. The beverage of choice for Karen was always wine, and the drug of choice was always prescription pills. Not the kinds that get you up, Karen could manage to get herself up very well on her own as she was somewhat manic to begin with No, the choice was the kind that brought you down, helped you forget what life had dealt you and gave you a sense of being. It had been a constant problem, usually brought on by events that shaped her emotional distress and at times when all hope seemed lost. While it was indeed a struggle, she did manage to control it, with lapses in-between as a result of her associations, but, nonetheless, she always came back to reality and knew it was important to keep straight for her son. She had managed it well over the course of the previous two years, especially since she was no longer involved with Ray. While Ray liked to consume his fair amount of alcohol and smoke his fair amount of "weed," he would always tell Karen she was a drunken drug addict, and that he was quite capable of controlling it for both of them. In essence, Ray would say, "without me, you will never be anything." The past two years offered her a different perspective on her own involvement and drug use, her relationship with men like Ray, and also opened her eyes to how you can be happy when "people are nice to you, and Maurice was nice to her." While Karen didn't quit drinking altogether, she did manage, for the most part, to keep it casual, and she only used prescription pills as prescribed to battle depression and anxiety that came from a gunny-sack full of bad memories.

Karen's relationship with Maurice was full of partying and outings with friends of them both in their professions. As her contentment and promise of a new and better life with Maurice, the life she had always dreamed of, took shape, she managed to overlook that Maurice, the doctor, was more involved in drugs than she realized. Doctors have a complete source of drugs, of any type, at their instant disposal, and they are pretty much free. Pharmaceutical Reps came in and out of the hospitals and the Doctor's offices as if there was a revolving door expressly placed just for them. They were the junkies of the industry and offered the professionals anything they wanted in an effort to get them to exclusively dole out their products. "You don't like this one, try this one. You like this one; I can get you as much as you want. Samples, Samples, Samples, that's what we are all about."

That was the nature of the beast in the medical industry, and, in addition to getting all the free "stuff" they wanted, they also received lucrative compensations for using the products. It was a "win-win" situation for the medical professionals. But, in many cases, and more often than is ever reported, it also opened the gates to a litany of problems, one in particular, being drug abuse by doctors. Maurice was one of those that started out "recreationally" just to see what it was like. It also relieved the stress of dealing with whiny and self-centered patients who felt that he was their sole property and should be available at every hue and cry. Most of the hue and crying coming from rich South Florida housewives whose husbands labored intently in the back-stabbing world they operated in to keep their wives in the laps of luxury, all the while taking business trips to the various exotic locations with their "secretary," wink, wink, in tow.

After a while, even the most patient and caring individuals in the medical profession can reach a point of complete and utter frustration. What starts out as getting involved in a profession for the purpose of making a difference and helping your fellow man would oft times become a slow pit of quick sand, and the more you struggled with it, the quicker it swallowed you up. It's no secret that one of the highest percentages of suicides comes from those doctors involved in the psychiatric field. And why not, how much pain and emotional discomfort should one have to endure hearing, how much whining and crying "poor me" should one have to try and fix, and how much frustration at the lack of results should one have to take?

When It's Time

Not generally the lack of results because you were unable to help, but moreso a lack of results because most people don't really want to be helped. You are their crutch and you are going to be their crutch for the duration, like it or not. It's not all that different with doctors in other fields in the profession as well. And Karen was about to find that out.

Rickie D. Maness

CHAPTER SIX - DIRTY LAUNDRY

    Karen was becoming very content with her relationship with Maurice. Perhaps, it seemed at times, too content. Karen's mother would come to her own condo in the area, which sat on the water overlooking the skyline of the Gulf, several times throughout the year, as she still lived in the D.C. area. The condo was originally owned by Karen's grandparents, the General, and was left to Karen's mother when both of Karen's grandparents passed away. Karen loved living there as it was always a place of solace for her when things got really bad. That was the main reason that Karen bought her house just blocks away in the same neighborhood. Not much for condo living, Karen had always wanted a house, in a neighborhood, and a husband that cared and supported her and one, that "was happy when I told him I was pregnant." Apparently, her informing Ray that she was pregnant with their son was not received as well as Karen had envisioned it would be. In fact, his reaction was one that left another deep scar on the psyche of Karen and added to the emotional baggage that she carried. It was also perhaps one of the reasons that she tended to overlook Maurice's detestable behavior with shoplifting, and helped her turn a blind eye to Maurice's elevation of alcohol and drugs. And the fact that Karen found herself getting more and more involved as well. But this was different, they could both control it and, after all, Maurice was a doctor, so he knew the limitations and would be readily available to help her if it got too out of hand, right?

    They enjoyed too many late night cocktail hours, too many weekend getaways that always ended up with excessive alcohol or drug use, but they always managed to pick themselves up on Monday and head back to their respective offices. There were also too many alone parties at the house between Karen and Maurice. Karen's mother started to realize that things were not going as quite as well as described and as forecast on the surface for Karen and Maurice, and tried to talk to Karen about it. Karen, feeling like she was trying to be controlled by yet another person in her life that she loved, started to pull away from her mother and ignored the warnings that mom was shouting.

Her mother even wrote Karen a letter describing how dangerous it seemed to be getting for Karen, how Karen was slipping back into a life of dependency and how costly it was going to be upon her relationship with Maurice and her connection with her son. She also knew that Ray would never get her grandchild as Karen had made sure of that through the legal process. (Later on, Karen had a Last Will and Testament drawn up prior to her mom and her taking a trip overseas. The Will expressly requested that under no circumstances was Ray ever to get any of her children.)

But the words and pleas fell on deaf ears, not by intention, but by design. Karen was finally at the doorstep of happiness and no one was going to get in the way of that, not Ray, not Mom, and not even what Karen knew was most dangerous, Maurice's issues with alcohol and drugs. They were planning to be married in the not so distant future. Maurice purchased a very large two-karat diamond engagement ring that he had specifically designed just for her. He treated her well and he was good to her son. Although he was Jewish, he helped Karen decorate the Christmas tree and celebrated Christmas with her for her son. He was not a selfish person and he gave Karen all she needed. It was going well, and the future seemed apparent. But like the ashes on the end of a cigarette in the wind, the future can disappear in the blink of an eye.

Karen realized that things were getting a bit hectic with the partying and the excessive "happy hours." But she once again felt helpless. She had a good man, a stable environment to raise her son who was now five years old and the communication between her and Ray had at least taken a turn for the better. Still, in the recess of her mind, a mind experienced at how quickly things can go from bad to worse, lay the fear of yet another tragedy unfolding. Try as you may to put things behind you, sometimes, you inevitably know that the road being walked upon has the proverbial pitfall. She wanted to curtail the partying on one hand, but on the other, she was still having fun, and that was something that she had not had in a very long time. And, on what seemed like just another Saturday night, Karen's future would be altered forever. Maurice and Karen had spent the day shopping for antiques, a lunch at one of the outside street restaurants, which of course, included several afternoon cocktails and a quick trip to one of the drive-thru liquor stores that were prevalent in this town.

When It's Time

After preparing a quick dinner for the son and getting him to bed, Karen and Maurice continued on with the evening partaking of wine, vodka and whatever else, just like many Saturday nights before. This night, however, seemed a little different to Karen. She couldn't quite put her finger on it. The atmosphere and Maurice's behavior were unfamiliar. Something was definitely amiss, and she was unsure of what exactly was going on. As they sat at the table late in the evening, Maurice suddenly, and without warning, started to drift off, became incoherent, and exhibited a confused behavior. He told her, when she questioned him if he was alright, that he was just feeling a little ill and perhaps he should just go lie down. Karen believed that he was getting a cold or the ever present flu that floats around South Florida this time of year and too much alcohol had added to his illness. After all, he was the doctor, and if anyone would know, he would. He asked her to help him into bed and she struggled to get him to the room, where Maurice became unconscious. Unfamiliar with this aspect, she became concerned, then panicked. She quickly got him to respond by yelling at him and shaking his face until he opened his eyes. She got him up, placed him the walk-in shower and turned on the cold water in an attempt to get him more revived. Maurice regained a semi-state of coherency and Karen took him to the kitchen table and made some coffee. As she sat questioning him as to what was going on, why he was acting like this and what he had been taking, Maurice confided to her that he had been taking morphine for the past several months to help him ease the pain of an injury. It started out slowly, but the necessity for a greater dose seemed to gradually creep up on him until he realized that it was suddenly becoming a problem. In an attempt to "withdraw" from the drug, he had started experiencing symptoms of severe cramps and nausea, but had managed to hide them from her over the past several days. Maurice eventually understood that he wasn't taking the morphine for pain, but moreso for the pleasure it gave. He had done quite a bit that day, throughout the day, and had taken a larger dose just before Karen put her son to bed. He told her to put him in bed again, and that to just keep an eye on him throughout the night. He assured her that he would be alright and would discuss it further with her in the morning.

Karen never had any experience with morphine, she didn't know that it was a time-release drug and, the longer it stayed in the body, the greater effect it had. Coupled with alcohol and other pain medications, it can be very lethal. As Maurice lay sleeping, seemingly struggling to breath, Karen became even more concerned, and even more panicked. She thought about calling 911 to have the medics respond but knew, given his position in the hospital and in that town it would most likely end his career. Several times throughout the evening she would go in to check on him. His breathing was sporadic and at times laboring. But then, on a few occasions, Maurice would talk coherently, albeit a little slow, to her about the situation. He again assured her he would be fine and that she should, under no circumstances, call 911. "It will absolutely destroy me" he told her, repeatedly. He made her promise that she wouldn't and, even though her fears told her she should not listen to him, the perplexing moment between "should I" or "should I not" bounced in her head like a ping pong ball gone awry. Eventually Maurice seemed to be resting comfortably and Karen sat on the couch, her fears ever present, but fatigued by stress, unable to keep her thoughts until she drifted off to sleep.

Karen was never able to tell me what time she awakened, knowing something was not right. She had that feeling of emptiness when you subconsciously realize that your world has suddenly changed in your absence and there is not a damn thing you can do about it. She quickly got up from the couch where she had remained and ran into the master bedroom. There, before her heart and eyes, her world came once again crashing down on her. She didn't need to touch Maurice, or search for a pulse, or even call his name to realize he was not of this world any longer. Maurice had died in his sleep while Karen fretted over what to do during the night. Karen started screaming hysterically, crying out to God to fix this awful mess, and, just crying. Her son, who was in the other room came in and saw her, and Maurice. He asked her what was wrong and she couldn't even tell him. She knew she had to call the police right away but wanted her son to be out of the house when they came so she called her mother first. In retrospect, this seemed the right thing to do, and in an effort to protect her young son who had seen his fair share of abuse and heartache in his young life. However, as it would later be a bone of contention, the police saw it differently.

When It's Time

    The police arrived, and shortly afterwards, the questioning began. Anytime there is a death of a "suspicious" nature, there are two things that the investigator looks for; motive, and opportunity. Since it appeared that Karen was the only one with the opportunity, the investigators went about to find the motive. Eventually the question of why she called her mother first instead of 911 surfaced. As police officers, we have to separate ourselves from the emotional side of an investigation and get a "Joe Friday" type of behavior; "The facts ma'am, just the facts." Well the fact that a person was found dead, the only other member in the household called someone else first, and not the emergency line, was not seen as the efforts of a caring parent to protect a young child from a vision that may haunt him forever, it was seen as an effort to cover up something. When an investigation starts with an assumed outcome, it is very hard for the investigator to be subjective and recognize things for what they are, not for what they appear to be. In law, facts, not assumptions, are what are most important, so, in this instance, the investigation got off on the wrong foot from the beginning. Add to an investigation a personal bias; let's say, the investigator doesn't like defense attorneys, it becomes even more difficult to conduct a proper investigation and come to a righteous conclusion. These things get in the way. Throw in the media and their well-contrived agenda, you have one big bowl of mixed up bullshit that can be slung around a community and eventually destroy lives, reputations and families.

    There was a song in the 1980's by Don Henley called "Dirty Laundry." It is the perfect representation of what the media mantra is and how they can use any story, sensationalize it in an attempt to get ratings or sell papers, then, when it is all said and done, move on. How many people have you known where a story was written or aired about something or someone you knew was not true, or at the very least, a partial representation of the facts? How many times have you witnessed the media, after learning the details of a story they went after with full vigor, only to find that they were not even close to uncovering the true story or the facts that would have shed a positive light on the individual, do a follow-up story admitting they were wrong?

You can probably count on one hand the number of times this has come to fruition. The media is in the business of creating news, not reporting it. Truth doesn't sell. Truth takes away from one's ability to imagine, pass judgment and give flavor to the miserable lives of those who are watching or reading. Truth, after all, is boring!

I was a victim of this myself as an agent for the Department of Homeland Security. I had an encounter with two police officers at a sports venue when I tried to intervene in a mistake they were making, after identifying myself, simply to let them know that the person they were accusing of doing something did absolutely nothing wrong and I was a witness. Suffice it to say that, three broken vertebra, three felony charges and a trip to jail ensued and it was front page news. It nearly cost me my career. Subsequently no charges were ever filed, one of the officers involved was later terminated for crimes unrelated to my incident and the other officer resigned and relocated. A law suit settled the issue after five years, but the press, not once, reported any truth to the incident. And the fact that the case was not filed on within a thirty day period gave them ample time to report that aspect of the case. They refused to do so and I was pointedly told that it wasn't news anymore when I tried to get them to. In the instance of Maurice's death, it would be Karen's first encounter with the press and her eye-opening experience of just how cruel, thoughtless and, even harmful, they can be. As one line in the song says, "kick them when they're up; kick them when they're down, kick them when they're up, kick them all around."

The press was brutal on Karen and initially reported her as a "suspect" in the investigation. The police were, for the most part, trying to do a thorough job and looking at all aspects, but the agenda had been set, at least on the part of one or two of the officers. It was also revealed that Maurice had purchased a small life insurance policy with Karen as the sole beneficiary a few months earlier. When approached with this information, Karen was surprised, as she had no idea. The policy, it seemed, was purchased without her knowledge and Maurice kept it in his office. He had planned on giving it to her as a wedding present along with some other things he had bought without her knowledge.

When It's Time

If not for the reality of the situation being verified by Maurice's office staff, it could have been portrayed as a Lifetime Movie epic. And of course, the Press ran with it from the onset.

Karen was eventually cleared in the death of Maurice, at least as far as the police were concerned. But she was never cleared in the mind of many in the town she lived in, nor in her own mind. Although Karen knew she was not responsible for Maurice's death, she would also carry the guilt and emotional burden of what if? "What if I had called 911 that night, perhaps Maurice would still be alive, although he would be ruined professionally by all accounts. What if I had known more about what he was taking and then I would have been able to keep him up and alert until the drug wore off? What if, what if? What could I have possibly done to prevent the death of a man that didn't deserve to die? And, why did he die and why am I still living? Why do I deserve to go on, and how can I possibly ever forgive myself to the extent that I can be happy?

These are the questions you find yourself repeating over and over for many years, almost on a minute by minute basis for the initial period after someone dies tragically and you feel you should have or could have done something more to prevent it. Second guessing becomes first nature, and you use the guilt to beat yourself up, sometimes almost to the point of submission, until you just can't function anymore in a manner that is beneficial to healing. Karen would carry this guilt with her in the gunny sack of emotional hurt and pain that life seemed to continually bestow upon her. She would carry this sack, even as it got heavier and heavier to manage, until she would someday transfer the sack to the one person she loved the most, and the one that loved her unequivocally, me.

Shortly after the death of Maurice, Karen was forced to sell her house and she went back to her roots in Philadelphia. She attempted to raise her son by herself and go back to school to entertain a career in medicine. She wasn't forced by the community, by the press or by anyone in particular, although they all had a hand in her personal feelings of guilt and destruction. No, she was forced by her own nature to once again move from a bad situation and hope to find happiness in a place where no one knew her past. Hard as she tried to escape the turmoil of yet another destructive event in her life, she was unable to do so.

Karen's time in Philadelphia was spent, for the most part, by drinking a lot to forget and going to doctors to get medication for her depression. She did manage to take care of her son, or, as it turned out, he managed to take care of her more than a young boy should. It was not a pleasant time for Karen, or her son, and in between attempts to get her life together and go to school, she would often return to her mother's condo in the town that she had grown to love, but had been very cruel in many ways to her. As time passed she was no longer the center of attention and Maurice's death became a foggy memory to most. The Press, of course, never ran a story about the final results of the investigation and Karen was fine with that as well. The last thing she wanted was more attention brought upon her. No, she anonymously came and went, visiting old friends occasionally, the kind of friends that stick beside you no matter what. They were few and far between so she really didn't have to spend much time socializing. Her mother would sometimes join her and, although quite concerned, once again, about her only daughter's future and emotional well-being, knew there wasn't much she could do other than to be supportive, both financially and maternally, and do what she could to ensure that her grandson was ok. Sometime around the Spring of 1998, Karen abandoned her attempt at returning to school, packed up her son, and went back to a place that had been the venue of much turmoil and hurt, but a place that, for her, was one where she didn't have to think about anything else. She reunited with Ray.

CHAPTER SEVEN - RAY- PART II

For Karen, returning to South Florida was bittersweet. It had always been a place that she wanted to live, but had also been the site of most of her turmoil over the past ten years. With the Philadelphia chapter being put behind her as an utter failure, Karen realized that she needed more in her life than just a fantasy about becoming someone else. She needed a reason to believe in herself once again; she needed a daughter, not only to give her responsibility and emotional comfort, but also to give her son a sibling that Karen never had. Karen never liked being an only child, and much of her childhood was spent in fantasy and with her mother, just the two of them. She was very lonely at times, inventing imaginary friends as a young girl to occupy her time, and, later on in her teen and young adult years, choosing friends that were less than desirable simply as a matter of having a friend. There were good friends, some that she still kept in contact with and shared many memories with; good and bad. But there were also those people that she thought were her friends but were far from it. The kind that are only your friend when things are going good or when they wanted to be a friend for what you could do for them, never returning the favor. It's a difficult lesson in life to learn that true friends are hard to find and even harder to lose.

Karen still clung to the belief that she was a good person, and she was, and still could not understand why life had continued to kick her about the way it did. Just once, she wanted something to work out to her favor and wanted someone to treat her the way she always tried to treat everyone else, everyone but herself. Karen was too busy feeling lost and alone once again to actually understand that people like Ray don't change their behavior, they just change their tactics. When she moved back to Florida with "their" son, Ray convinced her that he was willing to change, yet again, and that the years without her had made him see how much he missed her and wanted to "be a family." There was the magic word, "family," that which Karen wanted the most in life, but was never able to attain, and, the one thing that Ray knew would get her back.

Her relationship with Ray had grown cordial and Ray, in his manipulative way, gave her a shoulder to cry on and showed support to her and their son after the death of Maurice. Karen had maintained contact with Ray for the sake of their son, and maybe, as she would later discover, she always thought that most of the problems between her and Ray was a result of things she did, that Ray wasn't really that bad, and if Karen could just try harder she could have the family with Ray, the father to her son, and Ray, the soon to be father to her daughter. Karen never understood that this is how controlling and abusing men work; they only hurt you because they love you; and if you would just try harder to be better, they wouldn't have to hurt you to get you to understand. It becomes all about your faults, not theirs, and it becomes all about what you aren't doing, not what they are doing.

It is slowly ingrained into the psyche that the victim begins to believe it which leads to even more emotional guilt and self-flogging to the extent that they virtually become unable to exist unless they are in a relationship of control. Karen had not quite gotten that far down as of yet, but she was down far enough to where she was willing to give Ray another chance if he could only give her a daughter and be a family. Besides, she thought, maybe what Ray needs also is a solid family structure, and having another child might just be the anecdote that would give him the reason to change.

The day that Karen decided to leave Florida, again, with Ray, her best friend, the prosecutor that she started her career with many years earlier, learned of the departure. She quickly called Karen's mother and the two of them drove to the airport in Miami to confront Karen. Try as they may, they were unable to convince her that she was making a terrible mistake and that she should not leave, especially with Ray. A slight confrontation ensued between her friend and Ray, but even that was not sufficient for Karen to see what was about to unfold. Karen "knew what she wanted, knew what she needed, and knew she was not going to find it here." Somewhere, perhaps in the deepest recession of Karen's being, she knew that leaving with Ray was taking a chance. But, then again, Karen was always one to take a chance, and also knew what she wanted most of all.

When It's Time

Even in her depressed emotional state, and casting the bad memories aside, Karen at least had the wherewithal to protect herself in the event things turned out the same down the road. She left with Ray and shortly after became pregnant with the daughter she always wanted. Karen, in spite of her differences and past history with Ray, and in spite of her desire to have a child, a sibling for her son, never was comfortable with the "rotisserie father" scenario. She wanted her children to be connected by more than just the same mother; she wanted her children to be "total" siblings who would develop the bond that only those siblings could.

The facts surrounding the following months are not of significant importance. Karen left with Ray, they eventually moved to another country and she became pregnant. Ray had a job out of the United States and, although it wasn't the exotic location that Karen would have liked, it gave her time to experience a new life and to subject her son to a different culture. It also gave her time to escape the reality of the recent past and allowed her to concentrate on being a mother again. Since there was not a lot of opportunity to indulge in drugs or alcohol, things appeared, for now, on the side of normalcy. Prior to giving birth, in the last month of her pregnancy, Karen moved back to Missouri with Ray's mother while Ray finished the job he had outside the country. Karen gave birth to a beautiful baby girl in 1999 and Ray returned home to be with the family. And for six months, they were a family, or a reasonable representation of one. Ray had virtually exhausted the money Karen had received from the life insurance policy that Maurice had left her. He bought a truck and spent most of it on things that he wanted. Eventually every well runs dry and the relationship between Karen and Ray started ever so slowly to come full circle. Then, in the Winter of 1999, Karen once again was forced to flee the control and abuse that had again reared its ugly head.

On a blistery cold night, Karen loaded up her car with all she could fit, squeezed her son in the front seat and her daughter in the back, strapped securely in her car seat; surrounded by what little personal objects she could manage, and began the familiar journey back to Florida. Since, according to Karen, her and Ray had never married, this was the protection that Karen knew would give Ray little chance of ever having control over Karen through their daughter.

In order for Ray to ever get their daughter, he would have to prove Paternity and submit for visitation through the courts. Karen, being the legal mind that she was, knew that no court would ever give Ray that option, and, knowing Ray, he would never spend the money to try and do it. Ray never was financially responsible for their daughter either; another protection Karen afforded herself and her daughter. Ray did come back to Florida as well, after having the vehicle that he had bought with Karen's money, and was in her name, repossessed and refusing to pay support for their son. He had a few visitations with their daughter, but they were supervised visitations, since based on documents Karen had prepared, he was not to be alone with either Karen or their daughter. He also spent time with their son who was now older and knew the circumstances. This presented little opportunity for Ray to again take their son and leave. Since he was also greatly behind in support payments, he also knew that he would most likely be arrested if he did that, the one thing Ray did not want to ever be.

While Ray continued to try and control every aspect of Karen's life, he also knew that, in this venue, he was greatly outmatched. Although Karen had left Florida as a result of what some might perceive as a scandal (though it wasn't, it was just an unfortunate incident that had collected dust like all things the press make bigger than they are for sensationalism), she was still respected, surrounded by friends in the legal system and had more than a few allies willing to offer her protection should it come to that. Karen moved back into her mother's condo and Ray moved back to Missouri. This, for the most part, was the last connection that Karen and Ray shared as a couple and as parents. Now, in the throngs of loneliness and fear, once again, Karen began the struggle to put her life back together. She knew it was not going to be an easy journey, and one made even more difficult by the fact that she now had an infant daughter, no job, no money and no immediate prospects for either. She spent her days taking her son to school, which was just down the street, and caring for her daughter. She fought the desire to subject herself to drinking or taking medications, and she lived her life in normalcy, as normal as she could be, given the circumstances. But the one thing still missing in her life was love; not just love for the sake of love, but love given by someone towards her that was genuine and true, and the love she so desperately needed to give right back.

When It's Time

    Try as she may through casual dinner dates, which were few since most men aren't interested in hooking up in a permanent relationship with a single mom, especially one with a child so young, the love she wanted continued to escape her. Karen's life seemed destined for loneliness and hurt, garnered by memories of things that could have been, but, for life's interjections, were not. She had pretty much reached the bottom when it came to emotional stability and she spent her nights sad, disheartened, and on her knees praying to God for solace and comfort. Not being over religious, she believed in "a higher power," she never really had faith that her "prayers" would be answered, but continued every night, hoping that "something or someone up above" would answer her pleas and give her what she wanted so desperately. Then, one night in June of 2000, Karen fell once again to her knees, and simply asked, "God, please send someone to love me." That simple prayer would change Karen's life, and mine, forever.

Rickie D. Maness

CHAPTER EIGHT – US

September 19, 1996. That's the day that my life, unbeknownst to me, would change beyond what I ever imagined. It is so prevalent it is pasted in a frame on the wall of our house, along with some other artifacts, as reminders of that day. That's the day I had my first introduction to Karen Elizabeth Miller, Attorney at Law. The encounter seemed insignificant at the time, and in fact did not become significant for years to come. Sometimes, it just takes that long to "get it right."

I had always had friends that were attorneys, mostly prosecutors, but a few defense attorneys also. I learned years ago in my young career that one should not take things too personal when dealing with the aspects of the judicial system. I had even been called as an expert witness for a defense attorney friend of mine involving an ethics issue against a police agency. The agency involved, and the officer, had committed an unethical violation of the creed, and I was called to give the "proper" procedure in the investigative aspect of confidential informants. I always prided myself on my integrity and honesty concerning my job, and the defense attorney's that knew me well knew they could always rely on me to tell the truth, even if it meant losing a case on fundamental errors or some other habeas corpus event. Reputation in the law enforcement community is critical, and a bad reputation will follow you like a shadow on a bright sunny day. Or at least it used to be that way. Not so much anymore with the state our country is in. I have seen police officers do things that I, and those of my generation, would consider blatant abuse of our power, and worse yet, their agencies not only support them, but in many instances promote them. They then become the teachers and the cycle of abuse continues. While I wasn't perfect and made mistakes in my career, I was honest and very good at what I did. And that is the type of reputation a police officer should strive to have.

On this particular day, I was sitting at my desk in the Investigations Division of the Customs Office. I had been investigating an individual for transshipping computer chips from Thailand through the United States and eventually into The Netherlands. The Netherlands has a high Value Added Tax (VAT) on certain types of products that are imported into their country, and computer hardware was an extremely expensive one at that time. This was done not only as a source of revenue for a country that is the size of Rhode Island, but also to give competitiveness to those entrepreneurs that were doing business there. Certain flags were raised by the Dutch Customs when product was brought in from "source countries" that would indicate the product was of a specific nature and subject to the VAT. So, the proper labeling of products being shipped in was important in order to maintain that competitiveness and offer a fair playing field for all.

The individual I was investigating was purchasing computer integrals from Thailand at a discounted price, receiving them into the United States, then relabeling them and undervaluing the contents to avoid the high VAT imposed on items of this nature coming from Thailand. And, also to throw off the fact that the origin of the product was indeed Thailand. The Dutch FIOD, the Revenue Agency charged with investigating these violations, had contacted my agency to assist in the investigation. Several shipments had been seized by the FIOD as well as by us in Memphis, the hub for Federal Express, the company that was being used to send the shipments out. After several weeks of putting the investigation together I contacted the individual who was suspected of preparing the shipments and requested an interview with him.

Of course, as with all intelligent individuals who stand to make a lot of money in what we call the "white collar arena" this person was well poised in his answers and his alibis. After I expressed the seriousness of the situation, and the fact that the Dutch FIOD was so interested that they were sending two investigators to the States to assist us in the investigation, he quickly determined he needed an attorney.

When It's Time

On this day, September 19, 1996, the phone at my desk rang; the voice on the other end quickly identified herself; "Hello, this is Karen Miller, I'm an attorney representing Mr. Dicks. I understand that you talked with him and he has retained me to act on his behalf, so any future conversations with Mr. Dicks should go through me. And by the way, how many charges do you plan on putting on him?" I was taken aback a little by the abruptness of the conversation and, in all my years in law enforcement, I had never been asked a question about "how many charges" I was planning on indicting an individual for in the initial conversation with a defense attorney. My curiosity got the best of me and I asked her why she needed to know how many charges were involved. The answer given by Ms. Miller at first silenced me, and then I broke out in laughter. "I just want to know how much to charge this asshole" was her answer. Right then and there I knew I liked her and we arranged a meeting with her client at my office later in the week. I gave her the directions to the Investigations Office and we both ended the conversation with somewhat of a respect for the other.

Karen Miller showed up at my office, as arranged, with her client arriving shortly after in his own vehicle. We conducted the interview in the conference room, all the time her guarding her client's Rights like they were gold at Fort Knox. Realizing that this was just the initial meeting and trying to obtain as much superfluous information as I could get without stepping on the protection afforded a suspect, we had a good meeting and both Karen and I agreed that we would talk in the next few days. Over the course of the following week, we had several conversations, usually about the case initially, but we both realized that we were becoming friends and we enjoyed talking to each other as friends, but also as professionals. I did not delve into her personal life so, to be honest, I am not sure whether this time period was before or during her engagement and relationship with Maurice. All I knew was she was extremely intelligent, vibrant, petite, bubbly and a great pleasure to talk to. And, she was very pretty.

We garnered a mutual respect for each other that often times, during our phone conversations, turned from professional talk to talk in general about the justice system that we both had dedicated our lives to. I learned a lot about her as a person, as did she me, and I became comfortable talking to her on a personal basis, although neither one of us ever really got too personal. It was like we were just feeling each other out to determine where the investigation, and our lives, would eventually take us. We had one more meeting at my office a short time later, between me, Karen, another investigator and the supervisor. This was an attempt, on my part, to get her to understand the investigation, realize that her client was guilty as sin, and try to get him to take a plea to the charges, lessoning the penalties. I was unsuccessful in this venture because, Karen Miller above all else, was a brilliant attorney, and an even more brilliant litigator.

Karen was most comfortable in the courtroom and knew how to work the process. She also knew that juries were made up of, for all intents and purposes, people who led simple lives and had very little understanding of complex issues; As she told me when she rejected the attempts to get her client to agree to some sort of arranged plea, "This case is very complex. I am a very mart lawyer and I understand a lot of things, I am also a very good lawyer, and this case is confusing as hell to me. If I don't understand it, I am quite sure that a jury won't understand it either. And when juries don't understand things, they have a tendency to return a verdict that is favorable to the accused. So, unless you have anything more, I will be waiting to go to court."

So, I realized, it was up to me to get more to the extent that the investigation would be solid, fully knowing that this would take time, and that time would be used in being able to continue being involved with this wonderful person, Karen Miller.

About three weeks after our initial meeting, and after Karen and I had become somewhat friends, the Dutch FIOD investigators arrived. Armed with Judicial Warrants, we conducted a search at the office of Mr. Dicks. We also searched the office that Mr. Dicks had at the local airport where he was just venturing into setting up a flight school to train pilots.

When It's Time

Mr. Dicks, although not stupid by any sense of the word, was cunning to the point where he thought he could get over on anyone. He particularly thought he could "fool" the American police with his swagger and personality, so he agreed to a search of his residence as well. This search was not covered under the warrant so Mr. Dicks' consent was needed to conduct a search at the residence. Although I really didn't expect to find anything there, I utilized this process just to "screw" with him a bit and to let him know that the "American police" were not as susceptible to his cunning as he thought.

We arrived at his house with Mr. Dick's leading the way, and he let us into the gated community. The house was massive to say the least, and was in a very exclusive neighborhood right off of the Gulf. My first impression was, smuggling must be good. My second impression was one of envy, and maybe a little anger, at the contents inside the residence. The man had five Big Screen Televisions, one in each bedroom and the family room, this at a time when Big Screen Televisions were very new and expensive. I didn't even have a Big Screen Television, and I had a brother-in-law who sold them for a living and would have given me a great discount. He also had a Dodge Viper and a Mercedes 500 Class in his garage. So to say I was a little perturbed, although as I earlier said, you don't take things personally, was a slight understatement. In order to overcome my initial anger at this situation, I did the only thing I could think of at that moment, I called Dick's attorney.

"Hi, Karen Miller, you will never guess where I am. I am at your client's house doing a search." She seemed a little put off at first and immediately asked, "Do you have a warrant for his house?" Imagine my slight joy when I replied, "Oh no, we did have warrants for his offices that we searched, but not his house. He was kind enough to give us a consent to search his residence. Isn't that great?"

I don't know if it was my imagination or if the phone up to my ear actually started to get very hot and steamy. Karen called me a few names, most of what I don't remember, but the bottom line was, she was pissed. "Why the fuck didn't he call me, and why the fuck would you serve a warrant on his offices, and then get a consent to search his house, without notifying me. I thought it was clear that you needed to go through me to talk to him."

After these words, and a few other choice words, I simply replied, "But Ms. Miller, it is not my job to call you for me to tell you that your client's offices are being searched with a proper warrant, and it's not my fault your client is such a dumb ass that he didn't call you, and then gave us permission to search his residence. And, since I have not asked him any questions, he wasn't under the Fifth Amendment Protection of self-incrimination, sorry my dear." Needless to say, Karen Miller was quite upset and it took several weeks before she could actually see the humor in the whole event and also realized that, like I said, I was very good at what I did. In spite of her anger, she deemed me a worthy adversary and the respect we both had for each other grew even larger. I had not violated any confidence that she had in my trustworthiness, I was just manipulating the system the same way a defense attorney manipulates the system to protect their clients.

After one of our many meetings to come at my office over the next few months, I remember her walking out to her car in my parking lot. She had a swagger of confidence, yet alluded sexiness with every step. As she approached her car, she stopped, turned around and came back asking, "it's almost quitting time, would you like to go out and get a drink and some dinner, something to do out of the professional setting?" My heart skipped a beat, for, after all, not only had I grown to like her, and found her very personable and beautiful, I had no valid excuse for why I couldn't go, other than, I was married. My status as a married man had never been addressed and it had never come up before. I didn't wear a wedding ring, not because I didn't want people to know I was married, but because I didn't like rings on my fingers. In fact, I did not wear jewelry of any kind other than one gold necklace that was rarely visible and a watch I simply told her that I couldn't since I had some other things to do and left it at that. I don't know if she was confused, dejected or just slightly embarrassed. I only know that, in retrospect, I was glad I said no, but, also, looking back, maybe that day would have changed her life for the better for just a short while and led to her experiencing some happiness, however slight, that took much longer to find. But a relationship built on deceit is often a relationship built on shifting sands, and it can quickly develop into a relationship of distrust. So, as fate would have it in the long run, I made the right decision.

When It's Time

The case dragged on for months, since the Assistant United States Attorney involved with the investigation, as with Karen, could not quite comprehend the complexity of the scheme and kept soliciting us to get "more substantial evidence." Eventually the Government refused to prosecute, more likely based on the ineptness of the Prosecuting Assistant, and in direct correlation with the fact that the Dutch government was banging Mr. Dicks pretty hard in a monetary sense. Karen called it a win for her and for many years to come we would always wonder just how it would have turned out had we actually been pitted against each other in a court process. Dicks eventually got out of the computer parts business, after paying several million dollars to the Dutch government in penalty and taxes, and concentrated on his Flight School business. I didn't hear from Karen much after the case was dropped and the one or two times I did try to contact her at her old office number, I was simply told she was no longer at the firm. From 1997 to 2000, I would have no conversations with Karen Miller, and no knowledge of her whereabouts. She simply dropped off the radar screen so to speak, and had become an invisible memory.

The only contact I had from her was two years later in 1998 in the form of a phone message. I had returned to my office from lunch and my administrative assistant handed me a note pad with the message, Karen Miller called, she's in town and wants you to call her at this number. I hesitantly dialed the number, hesitantly I say because I was a little nervous about talking to her for various reasons, the most being excitement. I had often thought about her and how she was doing, where she was and why she just disappeared. I took the phone message, went to my desk, and with a bit of shakiness, dialed the number. The voice on the other end of the phone advised me that they had no idea who Karen Miller was and that I must have the wrong number. I repeated the phone number to them and was told that it was the correct number but they had never heard of Karen. Confused, I asked my assistant, who was in her late 60's, if she was sure of the number she wrote down. She told me she was and that the only thing Karen said was "ask agent Maness to call me. I'll be in town for a couple of days."

I called her old firm but was told they had not heard from her for over a year and a half and had no idea how to get in touch with her or any contact numbers to reach her. The last they had heard, she had moved to Philadelphia. Perplexed I set the message aside hoping she would call back. She didn't. As it turned out, my assistant had transposed the first three numbers of the exchange and I was never able to get in touch with Karen. Karen told me, years later, that she just took it that I didn't want to talk to her so she never called back and left town, again, thinking that no one cared.

CHAPTER NINE - FATE-OR DIVINE INTERVENTION

After my divorce in the early part of 2000, I became very depressed. I was in a large house by myself, with just my dog. I had no direction in my life and certainly was struggling to find a purpose. I began reading the Bible again, every day, looking for answers, or at least solace, as to why life would kick me in the teeth the way it did. I had just spent twenty years with a woman that, by all accounts, I believed, was the love of my life. Although we had grown apart over the past few years, comfort is one thing that people look for in a relationship, and I was, at the very least, comfortable. Apparently the same did not apply to my wife at the time and, as I said earlier, eventually she advised me she didn't love me anymore, wanted a divorce, and set about making it happen. Although we did go to "counseling," at her request and my agreement, I quickly realized through the counseling sessions that we were not there to attempt to reconcile; we were there for my wife's benefit of bringing out all of my faults, and to subsequently give her strength to get up and go. I walked out of the last counseling session we had and went to a Spring Training baseball game with a couple of friends. When I came home that evening, it was apparent the dye had been cast and that we were finished. I went and stayed with a best friend of mine, a defense attorney, and my wife moved out, leaving me with some furniture, the dog, and a dirty truck. My invitation to her brother's wedding which was upcoming shortly, was rescinded, and I was virtually cast out to be alone.

Being alone is good, if that's what you want. I personally have never been one who liked to be alone and found it very difficult. Throw in the emotional instability of just having your entire life ripped out from under you like a tablecloth in a magician's act, and the impact is overwhelming. In my mind, I had done everything my wife wanted. In her mind, I never did anything she wanted. I even got in my truck, with a friend of mine, and drove to Maryland and New Jersey just to get away.

My dog, my family, my job, meant very little to me at this point and all I could do was think about what went wrong, never realizing that, life, and fate, had a different role for me to now play.

The trip with my best friend, J.T., was horrendous and my mind became even more filled with thoughts of my life being over. I returned home only to find my divorce papers in the mail, which sent me even deeper into depression. Apparently the abyss between us was so deep that it could never be filled again, despite all my hoping and praying. I became so despondent that I went to a Psychiatrist who was a solace, but didn't have much to say. The talking was my responsibility. He prescribed me some sleeping prescriptions which I quickly abused, along with quantities of alcohol, and at one point, slept for three days straight. My soon to be ex-wife found out about this and called the doctor leaving a message on his voicemail. I remember walking into his office for my next appointment, groggy and lethargic, and him playing the voice message for me. He didn't ask me if it was true or not and didn't offer me the opportunity for an explanation, he simple looked at me and said "If you are doing this stop it. If you don't stop it, I will put your ass somewhere you don't want to be. Get your shit together, get on with your life, and get rid of your ego. Your wife left you, deal with it! I will help you deal with it if you want, but if you continue along these lines, you won't like the outcome."

He was a very large individual and an intimidating doctor, but was also straightforward, which is also the way I am, so it worked. Most of what he said seemed like professional rhetoric, but the "ego" word resonated. Although it wasn't an epiphany, it did start me thinking, and did get me to realize that, it really was about my ego being bruised. Over the course of the next two months I managed to get myself somewhat together and returned to work, found a home for my dog, and tried to get back my life which had been shattered. I didn't do much socializing and used the time alone to try and understand myself, and just what it was about me that was holding me back from having the "love" that we all desire. Sometimes, you can think you have it all figured out and you vow that you will change and do better the next time, if there is a next time.

When It's Time

Life has a funny way of bringing you back to reality, and God's compassion may take more time than you want to arrive, but it eventually does. Then, if you are willing, you can figure out the one thing you need the most to be the person you are capable of being. It took me awhile to figure it out, and I needed some fate, or as I believe, "divine intervention" to bring me to that place.

One of the things I enjoyed about my job as a Customs agent was driving tractor-trailers. I was one of a handful of certified tractor-trailer drivers and spent many hours on the road conducting undercover operations across the country. It gave me time alone and a peace that is found in solitude when driving. Since I was very good at it, I was often called to fly to various cities and engage in an operation as a driver. I don't remember the exact date, but I do know it was a Monday in early June, 2000. I had taken the day off, still trying to get the strength to actually exist for more than a couple of days at a time. I was sitting at the table, alone in my house, having a cup of coffee and reading my Bible. My supervisor called me to ask if I was coming back to work the next day. I said I was and he asked me, "How long will it take you to get to Omaha? They need you to meet up with another driver from Phoenix and drive a tractor-trailer to Newark, New Jersey in thirty-six hours." I told him I would get the travel arrangements made and depart as soon as I could. I flew into the airport at Omaha, Nebraska late that afternoon, Nebraska time, hailed a cab and asked him to take me to the Flying J truck stop about five miles away. There I met the other driver, a person that I had known for years and had been on training missions with, hopped in the cab, and away we went. Steve was a very good driver and, much like me, wasn't one for stopping once we hit the road. We knew the time restrictions we were under; the agents in Newark were waiting to take the truck and complete an investigation that had been ongoing for some time. We drove straight through, switching drivers while we took turns in the sleeper.

How it came about, I don't exactly know, but it did come as a memory flash in my mind or maybe a vision that entered and quickly left. As we were nearing the end of our trip, both being tired and restless to complete the journey, I remember driving through the outskirts of Philadelphia on the New Jersey Turnpike.

I saw the sign for the Philadelphia exit and suddenly, the name Karen Miller popped into my head. I had not thought about her for quite some time, being too busy dealing with my own mess of a life I had created, and I now couldn't top thinking about her, almost to the point of obsessing. Steve and I delivered the tractor-trailer to the Newark agents, went to our hotel rooms and made our travel arrangement to fly out the next morning. When I arrived back home, it was late, and I had a restless night. I wasn't sure if I was just road-weary or if I was just emotionally drained. I do know that I could not get Karen's name out of my head. The next day I called my friend, the defense attorney, and asked him to use his contacts with the Florida Bar Registry to find Karen Miller. This man had been a close friend of mine for many years. We were virtually inseparable for most of those years, and he was significant in helping me as I struggled through my depression after the divorce. He knew that if I was asking him to find Karen, it was important. Literally, within ten minutes, he called me back and said, "Karen Miller is still registered with the Bar and here is her address and phone number."

The address he gave me was the same address she had when I first met her, so I told him he must be mistaken, that she lived there nearly four years ago but the last I knew, she had moved to Philadelphia. "Well, I don't know about all that," he said, "But as of last month she was at this address and this phone number." I wrote them down and, recognizing the number he gave me, chuckled. It was then I realized the transposed number on the phone message my assistant had presented me with nearly two years ago. "What an idiot," I thought to myself, or maybe even out loud, "some trained investigator, you didn't even pick up on one number being out of place, the difference between where you live and where she lived." I left the store I was at when he had called me back and went directly home, clutching the piece of paper in my hand that contained her name and number.

As I sat in my living room, contemplating if I should call her, all kinds of thoughts raced through my head. "What should I say? What if she doesn't remember me? What if she's married, how will I explain the call? What the fuck do you want to do?"

When It's Time

    I knew the answer to the last question; I wanted to talk to her, find out where she went, what she had been doing and, most importantly, why she left without saying anything. But, the issue of her marital status became an obstacle in my mind. Since I never really knew if she was married or involved when we were friends, I could only assume that, "of course she has to be married. It's been four years almost, and a woman like that doesn't stay single long." Then I thought maybe she had gotten married and was now divorced. "But, it was only two years ago she tried to get in touch with me, she couldn't possibly have gotten married and divorced that quickly, could she?" As the anxiety of thoughts raced through my head, I quickly understood that, for some reason, I was supposed to call this woman. Maybe it was just another heartbreak looming for me, but, either way, I was destined to find out.

    I waited about an hour or so, had a beer, and since I wasn't much of a drinker to begin with, one beer would usually calm me down, and with sweaty palms, picked up the phone and dialed the number. I was hoping on one hand she would not answer, that I would get an answering machine telling me she was or wasn't with someone, and praying on the other hand that she would. The phone rang for what seemed like forever, and then she answered. "Hello, this is Karen Miller." Her voice brought me back to the times she would talk to me during our friendship. Wherever she was, she would always answer the phone the same way, "Hello, this is Karen Miller." It was a soothing voice, but still one of excitement. I paused for a moment then said, "Hi, is this Karen Miller the attorney?" She said, "Yes, this is Karen Miller the attorney, who is this?" Again, I paused slightly, not knowing how to approach the fact that I was not calling for official business, but also not wanting to seem like it was a personal call in the event she was with someone. "This is special agent Rick Maness, do you remember me?" "I remember you," she said. "What do you want?"

    At first it seemed a little curt to me and I immediately began to think she was with someone so I tried to keep it as professional, yet as friendly, as I could. "I looked you up and see that you moved back into Florida. I was just wondering" I paused, not quite knowing how to say the next line, "are you married?" Boy, I thought to myself, what a stupid question to ask someone right off the bat.

"No, I'm not married" she responded. "Are you engaged to someone" I continued. "No, I'm not engaged to anyone, what is it that you want, do you have a warrant for me or something? I didn't quite know how to take that question, actually being somewhat shocked that she would think that, and why? Knowing she was waiting for an answer I tried to give the best one I had as to the reason for my call. "I just wanted to know if you would like to get together and go out to dinner." Again, a slight pause, but one that seemed like a small eternity, and then "yes, I would, when would you like to go?"

If a heart can jump out of your chest, mine would have. The sigh of relief that I felt must have been heard all the way to where she was. "How does tomorrow night sound to you," I asked. "That sounds good, but I will have to get back to you to see if I can find a sitter for my children" she responded. The word children didn't even come across to me, and it would not have been an issue anyway. To Karen, the fact that I didn't immediately say, "children, oh, you have children, never mind" was a good sign. We agreed to meet at a restaurant halfway between where she lived and where I lived, about 20 miles in between, the next night, a Friday.

I must have seemed different when I went to work the next day. I had a different aspect about me. I guess, I glowed a bit, as my assistant would describe it. "Why are you so happy this morning?" she asked. "I have a date tonight with a beautiful woman" I said. We talked a bit about Karen and how I knew her, and of course, the fact that she had screwed the number up two years earlier, at which we both laughed. She was very happy for me and wished me well. That day dragged on and I remember leaving work early to go home and prepare, then I got the phone message on my house phone: "Hi Rick, this is Karen, I can't make it tonight; something has come up. I have to go be with a friend of mine who's having some trouble so can we do it another night?" Well, to say my heart fell would not do it justice. I immediately had all kinds of thoughts, most of them negative, about why she would cancel. "Maybe she changed her mind. Maybe she had second thoughts and really is involved with someone. Maybe she is just not interested after all. Maybe, she is still mad about me not calling her back two years ago." She said I could call her back but, since she didn't have a cell phone, she might not be at home but to leave a message anyway.

When It's Time

    I did call her back, and, as anticipated, got her answering machine. I tried to maintain my composure and not seem too dejected, and simply told her that I was fine with that and if she wanted to go some other time to just call. I gave her my cell phone number and hung up, fully expecting that I would not hear from her again. Then I waited. And waited, and waited. In the meantime, I decided that the only answer to the situation was to have a few more beers, and then I cried. I don't know why I cried, I guess the anticipation and excitement of actually going out on a date after twenty some odd years was quickly squashed in one phone call. The diminished aspect of having found her, only to have opportunity once again swept away, was an emotional bounce I was not prepared for. It was kind of like expecting your favorite toy at Christmas, and then opening the package to discover "underwear." I remember sitting on my couch, yelling at God, asking, "Why would you do this to me? Why would you give me some hope then take it away so quickly? Why?" I sat by both phones as the minutes, and then hours ticked away, finally realizing that she wasn't going to call, and I gradually fell to sleep where I had sat.

    The next day, Saturday, I found myself on the couch with a slight hangover and feeling extremely depressed. I had my coffee, sat at the table, again, questioning God and His "wisdom." I virtually moped around for the next two hours, trying to garner the strength to do something, including, calling Karen back. I picked up the phone a half dozen times, then, not knowing what to say, or more importantly, not knowing how I would take it if she didn't answer, or even worse, she did answer and told me she wasn't interested, but "thank you anyway." Then the phone rang, it was Karen. "Hi, I am sorry I missed your call, I had a friend that was having some problems so I spent the night at her house last night. Do you still want to go to dinner?" she said. "Yes, I do," I blurted without hesitation, maybe even loudly. "Ok, how about tonight, I have a sitter and we can meet at the same restaurant, say, around seven o'clock." Immediate glee is not the appropriate feeling I had, but elation would probably sum it up best. "I will see you there, do you need to know what I will be wearing" I asked. "No, I remember what you look like, I'll find you. If you get there before me, just sit at the bar as you walk in."

I hung up the phone, realizing that it was only six short hours before we would meet, and then feeling like it was six long days. I spent the next few hours contemplating what I would wear, what I would say, how would she look, what was about to happen, where was this going to lead?

Between four-thirty, and six-thirty that afternoon and evening, I must have tried on fifteen shirts and pants, trying to get just the right look. I didn't want to overdress but I also didn't want to seem like I wasn't one to take care of myself. After all, while not a real exclusive restaurant, it was known to be quite nice and shorts and a T-shirt were definitely not protocol. I settled on khaki pants, a nice pull-over shirt, shaved real well, used "the special" cologne and left the house at six-thirty sharp, planning the arrival at six-fifty. Meeting the time-frame exactly, I went to the bar, ordered a drink, and sat, and sat, and sat. Seven-fifteen came and went, then, seven-twenty. Now I was getting worried, and having no way to get in touch with her, negative thoughts started going through my head. The brunette sitting next to me continually engaged me in conversation. I tried to be polite and gave courtesy replies, but I was afraid that if Karen walked in and saw me talking to some busty brunette she would get the wrong idea. I kept one eye on the clock and one eye on the door. I also wondered if I would recognize her. People, especially women, have a tendency to change a lot over four years, so, that worry entered my mind as well. Then, at seven-twenty-five p.m. on that Saturday night, she walked in. Full of vitality, dressed in Capri pants, a tie-dyed T-shirt and flip-flops, she immediately walked up to me, gave me a hug, and said, "sorry I'm late, let's get a table." That was the exact time, place and day that I fell in love with Karen Elizabeth Miller, even though I didn't recognize it at the moment.

Karen and I spent that first night together, well at least most of it, in total ecstasy. Somewhere, around two o'clock in the morning, while I watched her sleep, I felt such love and desire for her that it frightened me. I didn't know what the future would bring, nor was I sure what was happening in the present. All I knew is that I had just spent the most intimate night with the most beautiful woman and suddenly I decided to leave, thinking that was the gentleman thing to do. I drove home in a blissful state, second guessing if I should have left or stayed.

When It's Time

The next day I sent roses to her apartment and tried calling her several times. She didn't answer throughout the day but called me back, seemingly a little perturbed, later that afternoon. She had awakened to find me gone, figured I had done the drive-by, and just left. She had been at the pool all day with the children and her friend Lori, and told me, "Honestly, I didn't think you would call me again." When I tried to explain that I thought I was being a gentleman, not wanting her to know that I was scared out of my wits at the prospect of someone like her wanting to be with me, she politely explained to me, "No, a gentleman would have stayed and been here when I woke up. But, the roses helped and I am glad you called me." Lesson Learned! The first of many that Karen would teach me about love over the coming years.

Rickie D. Maness

CHAPTER TEN - US, YET AGAIN

Karen and I became inseparable over the next few months, sharing our time between her condo and my house. The children, her son who was now eight and her daughter who just turned sixteen months, seemed to take to me and me to them. It was difficult at first. It had been many years since I had children around and sometimes I would get over agitated when I walked out of the bedroom in the middle of the night and stepped on one of the many toys that seemed to always be lying around. In time, however, I learned to be careful where I walked and to "just step over them" as Karen would often chide me. There were times when it seemed that I was being too hard on her son who I saw as a very intelligent young man, but one who often took full advantage of the "single-mom" phenomenon. Mom had been doing everything for him for as long as he could remember, and he was somewhat reluctant to pick up after himself. As we grew in our relationship, I found myself transitioning into being a father to the children, and although the role was very difficult, I thought I knew how to do it since I had raised my own daughter, Melissa, "Missi," from the time she was 13, who was now in her twenties with children of her own. Karen and Missi hit it off well, and Karen took on the new role of being a grandmother quite easily. As it would eventually turn out, Karen, aided by the self-absorbed opinions of her friends, eventually felt like my relationship with her son was one of contention. In retrospect, it was more about her friends protecting Karen from me, a person that none of them knew very well, than about protecting the children.

We became "officially" engaged in November of 2000, and planned on a February wedding. I remember the night I presented Karen with the question and her elation as we rode through the downtown area where she lived in her Chrysler LeBaron convertible, the BMW being a thing of the past. She immediately called Missi to tell her the news and they both repeated their joy. Karen, for finding what she thought was a man that truly loved her and Missi for her daddy finding someone to truly love and could truly love him.

Several weeks before the official engagement, Karen had related the events on the night before I called her, how she had sat on the floor in her bedroom, crying, depressed and praying for someone to "come and love me!" She wasn't sure if she was "praying to God, or praying to Maurice," but praying nonetheless. She told me that the next day, when I did call her she, "hung up the phone and stared at it for a while. Then, I became somewhat frightened thinking that this could be the answer to a prayer, which would indicate that there is truly a God, or this could be life getting ready to hand me another kick if you turned out to not be the person I wanted you to be." Fortunately, for both of us, at this moment in time, we had received what we prayed for and our love was growing by leaps and bounds every moment we spent together. Now that we were engaged, we were looking forward to the new chapter.

Right after Christmas, as the time approached for our wedding and the plans were coming together, things appeared to change in Karen. Subtle changes at first, a little depression and some forgetfulness, but then more dramatic. She was agitated by what she thought was me being too hard on her son. As it would turn out, it really wasn't her thoughts, but again more the thoughts of her friends. Her daughter, who had already started calling me "daddy," was going through the Terrible-2's and was a handful for both of us. I had already paid for our honeymoon trip to London, the place Karen wanted to go and a place I had never been. Invitations were sent out, the location for our wedding and the Pastor had been picked. Pastor Danny was a very knowledgeable and caring man and took to Karen immediately. He was the pastor of my church, the one I had been going to since my divorce and the one that Karen adopted as hers. Her relationship with Pastor Danny was one that gave her comfort, but always made her inquisitive about God and the "whole religion" thing. Karen and Danny had many conversations over the first few months prior to our planned wedding, and as it would turn out, solidified a relationship that lasted for a very long time. Then, about a month before the wedding, things took a turn for the worse in our relationship.

When It's Time

    The entire time that Karen and I were dating and into our engagement, I never saw Karen out of control, except one time. She never drank to excess or took medication with alcohol. But that started to change as the time for the wedding approached. She started spending more time at her place and hanging with one of her friends that, by all accounts, was a much messed up lady. Karen's mother had come down from D.C. to spend some time with Karen at the condo and, although her mother seemed to somewhat take a liking to me; I could also feel the hesitancy in her acceptance. It was understandable, of course, since she really had only what Karen told her about me to go on, and she knew that sometimes Karen made some bad choices in her relationships. So, the hesitancy was there and sometimes it presented an air of coldness when we were all together. I suggested that we, Karen, her mother and I, go to dinner. I would drive down, pick them up and go to Karen's favorite restaurant, The Outback. I arrived at the condo around six-thirty that night, and as I came in, I could tell that Karen was not her usual self; in fact, she was pretty much out of it. After a few minutes I decided that maybe we should not go out to dinner but Karen insisted since she had already arranged for her friend to sit with the children. Karen, I would later find out, often got her way when she wanted to go out.

    As I waited for Karen and her mother to get ready, I could sense that Karen was getting even more out of control. We went to dinner and attempted to have small-talk and conversation, particularly about the upcoming wedding. Suddenly, during the middle of the meal, I looked over and saw a very obvious panicked look on Karen's face. I asked her "Karen, are you alright, what's wrong." Karen couldn't talk to me, she was choking to death.

    At this instance, I have never been so afraid in my life. I knew what to do, but didn't know if I could "actually do it." I grabbed her from the booth, placed her on the floor and began to do the Heimlich to dislodge what was obviously a piece of steak in Karen's throat. I tried several times, all the while calling for someone to help me as it wasn't working. As the color in her face began to change and I began to scream louder, a gentleman approached, took Karen from me and, with two thrusts, dislodged the object.

Karen, very afraid, started crying, but she was breathing and alert. The individual said he was a fireman at the restaurant with his family and, although he insisted that we call 911 for an ambulance, Karen steadfastly stated she was fine and just wanted to go home. I never did get the man's name or where he worked, and I never got the chance to thank him. He simply got up and disappeared into the crowd that had gathered. I looked for him as we left but could not find him. I took them home, said goodnight, and drove back to my home.

The next day, Karen called me and, acting as if nothing happened, simply apologized for the incident. I couldn't let it go with a simple apology, however, and I felt the necessity to tell Karen how afraid I was and how much she scared me. I remember telling her, "Karen, what you did was very stupid. You have been doing some things you should not be doing. I will not watch you die. Last night scared the hell out of me, and I cannot do this. Either you get it together, or we are headed for some serious problems. Let me be very clear Karen; I WILL NOT WATCH YOU DIE!" I don't know if she took the words seriously or simply filed them in the back of her mind, but she continued in the funk she had fallen prey to.

Our relationship and our connection to each other seemed to slowly diminish. I didn't know what she was going through, but Karen seemed suddenly very afraid of getting married, afraid of how I would treat her children, and, quite possibly, very afraid of changing. One weekend, about three weeks before our wedding, Karen disappeared for several days with the friend that she had been spending more time with. I couldn't get in touch with her, did not know where she was, and she made no attempt to contact me. In spite of what had been happening over the previous weeks, I became very afraid that something terrible had taken place. I was finally able to get in touch with another one of her friends, the one who always knew where Karen was, and the one who was going to be the Maid of Honor for Karen. I called Lori.

"Lori, this is Rick; I haven't been able to get in touch with Karen. I don't know where she is, I haven't heard from her, and I am getting very worried." Lori told me that she had spoken to Karen a couple of days earlier and that she simply told Lori she was going to go away with another friend for a few days to get her head together.

When It's Time

I asked her just what was going on and she replied; "Rick, Karen is afraid. She doesn't know if she is doing the right thing and to be honest, she has some other people telling her that you aren't good to her children. I personally think you are but these other people are afraid that Karen will make a mistake and they are telling her these things. I've tried talking to her about it, but, she doesn't want to hear what I have to say. Karen has been through a lot, and she is very afraid."

The conversation ended with me asking Lori to have Karen call me if she heard from her, and also saying, "If I don't hear from Karen by tomorrow, I will gather all of her things from my house and bring them down there. I will drop them in your driveway and she can do with them what she wants. You can let her know."

As I had promised, without fanfare, and probably without even thinking, and even more out of anger, I loaded all of her personal belongings that had found their place in my home over the past several months into my friend's pickup, the defense attorney, and dropped them off in Lori's driveway. I didn't say anything, didn't knock on the door, just dumped them and left. While it may have appeared to be an immature thing to do, and in retrospect, it probably was, I felt that I needed to get Karen's attention and quickly. Time was running out. Two days later, after still not hearing from Karen, I cancelled the wedding with the Pastor, the Church and everyone we had sent invitations to. It was done. The only thing I could not cancel were the plane tickets to London, and as it would turn out, that would be a very good thing.

Karen, after being gone for nearly five days, suddenly, without notification, appeared in my driveway. With children in tow, and all of the things I took to Lori's house stuffed in the back of her car, she approached me in a frustrated, angered and yet, hurt state of mind. I remember her standing there, with the children, and saying "You're not getting rid of me that easy. You can't just throw my things out in the driveway and leave it at that. You're not getting out of this like that." After some bantering back and forth, we decided to go into the house and talk about it out of earshot from the children.

While Karen was very upset, she also knew that I had a right to also be angry. She explained to me her fears and that others were telling her not to do this, that I was bad for the children and that she should take some time to think about it. While she was also very, very angry that I took it upon myself to cancel the wedding, in the end she agreed that we needed to work some things out before we actually did get married. While our love was still strong, our approaches were coming from two different directions; Hers from one who had been hurt so many times that fear permeated her every thought for the future; and mine, from the angle that I knew all about love and how to be a father, husband, and all round good guy and couldn't understand why she couldn't see it.

In the end, however, we were both wrong, and we let our fear, or our "ego" intrude upon what had the propensity to be a beautiful thing. While the wedding was off, the Honeymoon was still on; after all, it was already paid for.

The flight to London was interesting. While Karen was still extremely upset at the cancelling of the wedding, she also knew that, for now, maybe it was a good thing. It would allow us time to understand each other more, put aside our fears, and ego, and give us time to develop a stronger relationship. We had never been anywhere, alone, together, without children or some other couple, so, this could be a great opportunity, or test, of our love. The seven and a half hour flight over the Atlantic began smoothly, but once we crossed the halfway point, Karen decided to air it out. And airing it out meant, having a few cocktails. While we had some deep discussion about each other's feelings and what we wanted individually, I could still sense that she was being extremely guarded in her approach. You see, what Karen wanted was assurance; assurance that she would not be hurt; assurance that her children would be loved and cared for, and assurance that I was going to be the person to provide her the "family" she always wanted.

What I wanted was assurance that Karen was going to be there through the good and the bad, and that every time something came up, as it undoubtedly would, she was not going to run or resort to familiar behaviors that always resulted in bad decisions.

When It's Time

Things were going pretty well until the Flight Attendant brought the British Customs Declaration around to fill out. She asked if we needed one, or two? I said two, thinking that since we were not married we would each have to complete our own. I had never flown overseas with anyone, only by myself. Karen, who had flown many times overseas with her mother, of course, said one would be fine since we were travelling as a couple. By my asking for "two," Karen took it as we are not a "family," which of course created a hostile attitude and some harsh words. It went downhill from there.

After we landed at Gatwick Airport and approached the British Customs area, the Customs Officer at the window to the Passport area took our passports from us and asked, in perfect Queen's English, "What is the nature of your visit, business or pleasure?" I stated that it was pleasure, and after seeing that the names on the passports were different he continued, "And what is your relationship?" Before I could get the words out, Karen, in a terse voice with agitation showing on her face blurted out, "At the moment, very strained."

Without looking up from his window, the Officer stamped our passports, handed them back to us, murmured good luck, and sent us on our way. While it did seem rather hostile and awkward at the time, Karen and I would laugh about that for many years to come as we imagined that the Customs Officer was thinking, "Strange Americans, and poor Lad, hope it all works out." We left the airport, took a Black Cab to our small, but quaint hotel in the Soho district, and proceeded to chart our next five days. I had recently conducted an investigation with officers from the London Serious Fraud Office (SFO) and had arranged to meet the two officers and the female Barrister, Claire, the next day for some sightseeing and socializing. So that evening, we decided to just explore the local area.

Since it was February, the weather was rather chilly by our standards. In fact, it was downright cold to us. Karen had brought her fur coat with her, which was given to her by her grandmother on her mother's side, and couldn't wait to get it on and walk around with it. She, herself, would never have purchased a fur coat, but the fact that it was her grandmother's, and that she had little opportunity to wear it in Florida, she was excited about wearing it. We took off for some exploring on foot, her in her fur coat and jeans, I in my medium sized coat and khaki pants.

The tenseness of the flight and the incident at the airport had subsided and we, whether intentionally or not, began to have a good time and began to be a couple in love. As we walked through the small cobblestone streets outside the hotel, we came across a quaint Pub and went inside. There was a large open-hearth fireplace in full operation and the atmosphere was very cozy. We had a couple of local beers, talked, laughed and, since there was virtually no one in the Pub at this time, enjoyed the solitude and the fact that we were together. We then went shopping, our first stop being the Doc Martin Boot Company. Karen had two pairs of Doc Martins at home, and had worn them for the past ten years, still intact, and still her favorite boot to wear. But, this was London, home of Doc Martin; she had to buy another pair, here.

The three and a half hours at the Doc Martin Store was excruciating for me, since they had no elevators or "lifts" as they are referred to there, and we had to visit every floor, several times. She finally settled on a nice basic black pair of Doc Martin boots and we started the trek back to the hotel. I asked her if she was going to wear them as we left the store and she replied; "Of course not I can't wear them until I get home." I didn't understand the logic, but later on, it would be explained to me in the most unorthodox manner. When we arrived back home, Karen took her new pair of boots, put them on, and walked into the hot tub where she stood for several minutes. Apparently, this is how you "break them in" and make them fit. I had never heard of such a thing.

We ventured back to the quiet and quaint little Pub we had visited on our way out from the hotel as it was getting dark and a bit colder. When we got there, the Pub was packed and it was all we could do to get in the door. We managed to find a little table off to the side after a few minutes and we ordered a couple of drinks. People around us, realizing that we were Americans, began, one by one, to talk to us and displayed an atmosphere of total acceptance and relaxation. Karen had that effect on people of any venue. Then, someone came in and said it was snowing outside. The entire occupancy of the Pub went out to the square in front and we all stood there in the snow and having a good time.

When It's Time

It was a most beautiful site and, as I looked at Karen, in her fur coat, laughing and displaying that beautiful smile, twirling around and joking with the other patrons, I suddenly realized that I wanted to spend the rest of my days with this woman. She brought light to everyone she met and to every place she was, and those "foreigners" around her were enjoying her company as much as I. After finishing our drinks, we went back to the hotel and spent a romantic evening alone. For the first time in a long time, we were truly in love.

The next few days were excitingly romantic a we traipsed around London visiting all the magnificent places that this wonderful city has to offer. We grew closer with each Black Cab ride, Double Decker Bus trip and just strolling to various places to take in the local cuisine. When it came to navigating in a city, even one such as London, Karen was indeed the Lewis and Clark of the trip. Give Karen a map, or a bus route, and she could get you anyplace you wanted, or needed to go in effortless fashion. We met my friends from the SFO and had lunch at the Superior Court in London in the chambers that only the judges and barristers, and invited guests, are permitted to eat. We visited other places around the city and had lunch in a magnificent pub in the heart of London. Everyone that came in contact with Karen was immediately struck in awe by her grace, her intelligence and her wit. She truly lit up a room when she smiled.

I remember being in a large Pub probably a century old and completely authentic that had a giant open floor, what seemed like a never ending bar made of beautiful wood and watching Karen "hold court" with a half dozen of the investigators from the SFO. As I excused myself to go to the restroom, which was located in the upstairs portion of the Pub, accessible only by climbing an abundant set of stairs that curved to the middle from each side of the bar and met in the middle with a huge oak railing overlooking the center of the Pub, pausing and gazing down below.

There, in the middle of the room was Karen, sitting on a barstool surrounded by the eloquently dressed members of the Office, some complete with umbrellas at their side, all appearing to be mesmerized by Karen's conversation.

I stopped for a moment to take it all in, and once again, became overwhelmed at how this beautiful woman could captivate the attention of anyone, and her laughter and smile enlightened the hearts of those she touched. I considered myself very lucky to be the man that was chosen to engage in a life with her.

We concluded our trip with a visit to two individuals that Karen had met in Turkey several years earlier and shared an apartment in London. They had become, and remained, friends over the course of the next few years and Karen had told them of our coming to London. We had a marvelous visit, toured the city at night in the Honda Accord that Lenny owned, which in itself scared the hell out of me. I had to sit in the back while Lenny drove, and, with the steering column being on the "wrong" side, it was a truly frightening ride. We left the next day to return home. On July 7, 2001, Karen and I were married.

CHAPTER ELEVEN - A LIFETIME OFFICIALLY BEGUN

Our wedding was beautiful and held at an old Historic Landmark Home, with its massive expanse of wrap around porch, gardens filled with various flowers and tropical plants, nestled up against the flowing water of the river running through our city. Our Pastor, Pastor Danny conducted the ceremony and my best friend, the defense attorney, as well as "Snake," an overpowering individual with the heart of a kitten, were my two Best Men. I had chosen Snake and the defense attorney because, through all of the turmoil that I had been through in my divorce, they had always been there to help. Snake and I were on the Sheriff's Department together until he left to go to a state agency. J.T., my other best friend, had moved to Maryland, again, to try and get his own life back together after he came home one night and found his wife had been involved with another man. My younger brother, Dave, would have been the logical choice, had he not been Best Man at my previous wedding. Somehow, they tell me, that isn't good luck. Dave and I were, and still are, very close.

All of our family and friends were there, and, as usual, Karen absolutely glowed with beauty and warmth. We both felt so blessed to have found each other, particularly in the manner that we did, and we were anxious to begin our new life together. July 7, 2001, was probably the happiest day of my life, and I know it was hers as well.

In spite of our bliss and happiness, to say that Karen and I had reached a point in our relationship where everything was great would not be truthful. As with any couple entering into a marriage, even moreso those at our age and with "step-children" being part of the package, there is always a bumpy start. Yes, we had been living together off and on for the past year. It was I that insisted that we get married if she was going to live full-time with me. I knew how awkward it is for children in a situation such as this and I insisted that we would not put the children in that box. Her daughter, Zoe, now my daughter, was calling me daddy.

Her son, Griffin, now my son, called me by my first name but always referred to me as "his dad" to others. Griffin had not had much contact with Ray since Karen and I became engaged, and Zoe had no contact whatsoever. This was not my doing, but more of an attempt by Karen to protect her children, and subsequently me, from Ray, knowing that he and I would definitely have differences should we meet. And the outcome would not be favorable to Ray.

The only time I had ever laid eyes on Ray was when he came to my house to pick up our son just before we were married. He had planned a trip for him and Griffin to the Keys that had been established early on in Karen's and my relationship. Even then, Ray tried to manipulate and control the process by insisting that Karen meet him with Griffin at some remote location. Karen refused and held steadfast to Ray coming to "our house" to pick him up. Ray would get angry, say he wasn't coming, which truly upset our son, then a day later would call back and say he was coming but, again, not to the house. This game ensued for several days until Ray relented and agreed to pick up Griffin at our house.

I remember standing in the garage when Ray arrived. He pulled into the driveway, but not all the way in, opened the door and let Griffin get in the back seat. He was a tall handsome man, but his outward appearance exuded anger. His demeanor was one of frustration and manipulation. Karen was in the driveway a few feet from Ray holding Zoe, who was just under two years old at the time. I saw her hand Zoe to Ray as he stood by the driver's door with one foot on the ground and the other perched inside the vehicle, as if to be determined not to give all the way in to Karen's demand that he come to the house to pick up Griffin. Immediately upon Ray holding Zoe, she started screaming and Ray gave her right back to Karen. He then yelled something at Karen for a moment until he saw me standing there. He quickly got into the car and left. That, to my knowledge, was the last time Ray ever had anything to do with Zoe. As Ray left our house at an accelerated speed, I asked Karen what he was screaming to her about. "He just wanted to make me feel like shit one more time by telling me that it was my fault that he had to come here to pick up his son, and that it was my fault that he doesn't have anything to do with his daughter. Everything is my fault, he never does anything wrong."

When It's Time

That was the last time I ever saw that man, and have never spoken to him, ever. Ray did try to continue to make Karen feel bad about things over the course of the next two years, however. He would send her text messages, especially on his birthday, telling Karen what a mean and horrible person she was. I don't remember him ever sending her a text wishing her well or asking about the children. It was all about how bad she was and what a wonderful person he had been to her. The first year after we were married Ray did send a box of Christmas presents for both of the children, but that was the last time. There were never any birthday cards for them or gifts of any kind over the course of our marriage, and the trips with our son ceased as well.

After the second year or so of Ray's occasional nasty text messages, I had finally reached the end of my patience with Ray. He had sent a text message to Karen, again, basically saying that she was a piece of shit, and that what she was doing was wrong. It was a lengthy message full of negative wishes and condemnations of Karen as a mother, a wife and a person. I took Karen's phone, replied to Ray that I had had enough, and should he continue with these "messages," he would not like the outcome. I invited him to call me to discuss it, but he never did. From the tone of the text, it appeared that Ray had gotten his courage from the bottle that night. Karen later told me that on holidays and his birthday, he always got drunk and became very mean and violent. Oh, there were texts between Karen and Ray over the course of the next few years; Karen would always text him when she started feeling guilty about her life, and Ray would always text her to let her know he "was still around." But there was no more contact with Ray since that day in our driveway.

I once became concerned about her "texting" Ray and asked her if she had any regrets about not raising her children with Ray since I knew how important the family structure was with him. Karen told me, with pure sincerity, "I don't hate Ray because of what he did to me, a snake is a snake. You can't change that. I hate me for what I let him do to me. To be honest, Ray is the only person in this world that I could shoot, and then go have a drink. That's how I feel about him."

Karen, although holding on to this feeling about Ray and her own feelings about herself, and what he did, never let the children know her mindset. Neither Karen, nor I, ever said anything negative about Ray to our daughter, and our son, having lived through a part of it, never had to be told. When our son became a teenager I told him that if he wanted to have contact with Ray he was welcome to, that I would not be offended or hurt. He simply replied, "I don't have anything to say to him. I'm fine." Whether he "was fine" or not is something that only he can determine, and how he deals with the events that transpired, and were still yet to come, will be a challenge, as it would be for any young man of his astute character. As for our daughter, having never had any contact with Ray that she could remember, only has to deal with the stories she heard from others, and the fact that Ray, in all her years, never had anything to do with her, not even on a casual, once a year on her birthday, basis. She now understands why Karen felt the need to protect her, what she doesn't understand is why Ray never made an attempt to change and be a man that, at the very least, would send a simple birthday card.

After our wedding on July 7, 2001, Karen and I went to Costa Rico for our "official honeymoon. I was just getting ready for surgery as the result of an accident I had at work and walking was very difficult. I remember going to the La Fortuna Waterfall near the Arenal Volcano with Karen on one of our excursions, looking up at the very high, and what seemed to be, very rickety stairs, and thinking, *"wow, she's not really expecting me to climb this?"* She was, and I did, and Karen exhibited great patience while I did. I remembered that Karen had often told me the most innocent way to get rid of someone was to take them hiking in the mountains. *"Was she really still pissed about the flight to London" I wondered."* I took the chance and climbed the stairs.

Our five-day trip to that beautiful country was wonderful and shortly after we returned home, I had surgery to repair my hip which resulted in several weeks of convalescing. Karen had now become employed full-time at the Public Defender's Office in our hometown and quickly jumped to the felony division after a very short time in the Misdemeanor Division.

When It's Time

While she truly loved her job, and adored and respected her boss, *"The"* Public Defender, she had a hard time transitioning from the fast-paced, high volume cases of Miami to the laid back, cavalier attitude of the courts here, and the types of cases that they actually deemed serious.

Karen would often come home and tell me about a case she was defending where an individual had been charged with multiple felonies and was looking at a very long time in prison if convicted saying, *"In Miami, this case would have been pled out to a lesser charge months ago and would never have seen the inside of a courtroom."* Here, the police over-stack charges, the Prosecutors file on everything they are given, even if it isn't factually true, and no one seems to care." She just could never understand how the system allowed certain things to happen here, a smaller city, than in cities like Miami, or Tampa, where Karen also spent a brief time as an Assistant Public Defender. The disparities were very hard for her to adjust to. And, being the litigator she was, and with the experience she had, she quickly became well known and respected in the court and law enforcement settings in our town.

One afternoon I was sent to the Coast Guard Station at the beach to assist in the detention of some Cuban refugees that had been intercepted by the Coast Guard trying to make their way to one of the outer islands that dot the coastline. As I was sitting there with the deputies from the sheriff's department, the department I used to work for, waiting for the Detention Officers from Miami to come over when one of the deputies said I looked familiar. I told him my name and he immediately said, *"Oh, you're Karen Miller's husband."* I turned to my partner and said, *"Over twenty-five years in this town as a law enforcement officer, and in two short years, I've been relegated to being "Karen Miller's Husband." Isn't that just appropriate?"* Another example of how popular this woman was. When I told Karen about the encounter she laughed and from that day forward she always referred to me as *"Karen Miller's husband."*

While Karen very rarely used my last name in her professional setting, I'm not sure if it was to protect me or allow her to make her own legacy, she would invoke it when needed. There were times when she would come home and ask me if I knew a particular deputy or police officer that she had just had a deposition on. When I told her I did, she would usually say something along the lines of, *"I had a deposition with him today and he was being a real jerk and not wanting to answer questions and had a smug attitude. When I casually interjected your name into the conversation and that I was married to you, things changed and he answered all my questions and said to tell you hello."* Like I said, both Karen and I had good reputations in our town and in our professional demeanors.

Karen was also a Board Certified Criminal Trial Lawyer, an honor that is bestowed upon those attorneys that have a proven record of trial experiences and successful peer reviews and accolades as well as an arduous s six hour examination on competency and knowledge. Karen was very proud of this Certification as she was the only one in the Public Defender's Office to have attained it, and one of a handful in our town to have achieved this feat. Her own boss, the Public Defender, had taken the exam several times prior and could not pass it. The first time Karen took the exam was three days after she had just had major surgery and was in the hospital for two days. Her boss was taking the exam at the same time. Karen, as expected, passed it on the first attempt.

Respect and notoriety can be strange bedfellows or best friends, depending on the perception and who's doing the perceiving. In Karen's case, her notoriety would eventually become her enemy, and her respect would be often challenged by those who saw that respect as a threat.

September 11, 2001! Everyone who is over the age of twenty knew where they were the day of September, 2001, or, 9/11 as it has come to be known. When the Twin Towers in New York City were attacked and eventually collapsed, I sat on my couch, recovering from my surgery, and cried. I grew up looking at that skyline, one of the most remarkable skylines in the world. I even stayed in the hotel on the bottom floor of one of the Towers, and spent two occasions on temporary duty there as I completed an investigation that led me to New York City.

When It's Time

Our Customs Office was in Building Number 6 and was totally destroyed as well, although all of the employees in that building managed to get out safely before the Towers fell. Karen called me from her office to tell me about what had happened but I had already been watching since 9:15 that morning. She came home that night and the two of us sat glued to the television through the late hours and resumed it the first thing the next day. Although she didn't want to go to work she had some hearing to attend to and did manage to come home rather early in the afternoon. I am not sure if it was the next evening, the 12th, or the following evening, but, as we sat watching the numerous broadcasts of the major networks, a familiar face appeared. A reporter was interviewing the individual that had operated the Flight School that trained two of the pilots that flew into the First Tower. There, in all of his arrogance and bullshit, was Mr. Dicks.

Neither of us could say a word as we watched this man on television, knowing full well that his connection to us was that he brought us together, inadvertently by hiring Karen as his attorney, and that by the U.S. Attorney's Office not prosecuting him, he was allowed to continue his business here and subsequently train these horrendous terrorists. Over the course of the next year several agencies tried to make a conscious connection between Dicks and the terrorist students, but were never successful. Dicks would come onto my radar screen several years later when he attempted to bring in some grey-market" motorcycles from Europe or Central America, someplace where the motorcycles were not allowed to be brought into the United States. I received great satisfaction in notifying our Orlando Office and having them seized. Although there was no criminal prosecution, it cost him time and money and put his name on "the list" of people who have tried to smuggle items into the U.S.

Several years later Karen would come home and take great joy in telling me that Dicks had been arrested for attempting to smuggle drugs into the U.S. someplace in Texas. Although she didn't know the city or the facts, and we never found out the outcome, both of us felt somewhat vindicated in our association with Mr. Dicks.

Over the next two years, Karen and I went about solidifying our marriage and our family. We were very much in love and her career was beginning to take off. Karen, being the brilliant attorney she was, coupled by her radiant personality, made friends in the office quickly and the respect for her grew. Since her office and mine were both in the downtown area, we would spend a lot of time having lunch together. Sitting in a downtown restaurant one day, a group of people from her office came in, led by a tall busty female that I recognized from my years with the local sheriff's department. She saw Karen sitting with me and waved to her. Karen smiled, waved back, and we continued our conversation. *"Do you know that person?"* I said to Karen. *"She's my supervisor"* Karen replied. Seeing concern on my face she asked, *"Do you know her?"* I simply told her I knew of her and offered a suggestion, *"just be careful of her, she has quite the reputation."* We dropped the subject and, as it would eventually turn out, had my words been heeded, things may have worked out differently.

Karen grew to have great respect for the Public Defender at that time, a man whose devotion to the office and his employees was coupled by his desire to give everyone the benefit of the doubt. While not the overt ball of fire that Karen had been accustomed to in the larger offices she worked in, he took a great liking to Karen and made sure that she was on the right track to succeed. He continually gave her great responsibility and, at every opportunity, made sure she was recognized for her work. When he passed away several years later, Karen took the loss very had. She kept a framed photo of him on her desk for many years to come and praised his abilities as a lawyer and his compassion as a person to everyone who saw the photo and inquired about him. He was a champion for the underdog and a compassionate person, the qualities that Karen could relate to the most.

CHAPTER TWELVE – LOYALTY

    From the time we were married in 2001 and up to November, 2002, I never saw Karen drunk or emotionally out of control. We would enjoy a glass of wine together, although I detested wine, every so often at night, and we maintained a very good relationship, and marriage, for that period. Karen was becoming more and more at home in this town and in her job. She was making friends in the community, the neighborhood, and in particular, her office. She quickly, to my discontent, became friends with her supervisor, the one that I had warned her to careful of. Karen had several things she cherished, but the most was the necessity to have a "best friend." Funny thing about best friends, they always seem to be your best friend until you really need them, then, they quickly dissolve into "acquaintances," not in all cases of course, but in many. Both Karen and I would learn this over the course of the next few years, my education in this regard coming rather quickly, and Karen's to follow down the road.

    Things were going well as we celebrated our Anniversary and entered our second year of marriage. We enjoyed time together, going to football games where we had season tickets, motorcycle rallies and Poker Runs, and, just being together raising the family. My third grandchild was born and Karen was there for the delivery. The happiness on her face holding that child was elating. But there were some rough patches also. Karen had ovarian cancer and had to have a partial hysterectomy which quashed any plans for us having a child together. She also had a medical problem that resulted in some other surgery to remove her gall bladder. But through it all, we stuck with each other and continued to forge our bond. In November, 2002, Karen got arrested for a DUI, Driving under the influence, and things seemed to turn for the worse for the next two years.

    It was a Sunday evening when I got the call. I had gone to the football game in Tampa with a friend of mine. Although Karen and I went to most of the games together, there were times when I would take a friend or Karen would go with one of her friends.

On this particular day I had gone with a long-time friend, a man that I had been on the department with years earlier, and a man who also was friends with the defense attorney, my best friend, and a Best Man at my wedding to Karen. On the way home my phone rang and the defense attorney advised me that another friend of ours, a Captain on the Department, called him to say Karen was being arrested and asked him to get in touch with me. She was less than two miles from our house and had been coming home from an afternoon with her mother and the children at her mother's condo, thirty-two miles away.

I immediately called the Captain, who happened to be on duty as the Watch Commander at the time, and asked him what was going on. He told me Karen had been arrested and they were waiting for someone to come and get the kids. Since I was about an hour away, they couldn't wait for me. I remember asking this Captain, a person that I had known for over twenty-five years, had been his Training Officer when he first came on the department, were Sergeants together in the same division, was at our wedding, and had just gone on a cruise with Karen and I, and the defense attorney, several weeks prior, if he would go out and check on Karen to make sure she was ok. My first taste of what loyalty to friendship really was, or was not, about, was when he refused to go and told me, "I can't get involved." The only thing he offered to do was let whoever came for the children also take the vehicle, my vehicle that Karen was driving, and not have it towed. "Way to step out and be a friend," I thought. But then again, he never really had any balls anyway.

Needless to say, Karen was arrested, refused the Breathalyzer, as all good defense attorneys do, and was taken to jail. When I bonded her out eight hours later, that's the law, I was so angry that I simply did not talk to her. In spite of Karen's insistence that she was not drunk, had only had one drink at lunchtime, some six hours earlier, I still had it in my mind that the police don't make mistakes like this. Call it old habits or professional indoctrination, but in my mind, she must have been drunk or "they wouldn't have stopped you." It was nearly ten days later, when I finally obtained a copy of the video tape that her attorney had received of the stop, the Field Sobriety Test and arrest, that I learned another valuable lesson; things aren't always what they seemed.

When It's Time

As I sat in our living room, while Karen was at work, watching the nearly fifty-five minute long tape, I knew immediately that Karen was telling the truth and that something was terribly wrong. Karen, indeed it appeared, was stone cold sober.

The ramifications of this arrest would test the friendship of me, the defense attorney best friend, and the loyalty of Karen's peers. Having some adequate experience in the investigative aspects of traffic offenses, I went about conducting my own investigation including travelling the thirty-miles or so from her mother's condo, through all of the multiple traffic construction sites that caused vehicles to have to maneuver carefully, the stop site where the field sobriety test was conducted, and the paperwork associated with the stop and arrest. My conclusion was that the arrest was bogus, permeated upon saving face of the female off-duty officer and her husband, the officer that made the arrest, as well as my concerns about political implications.

As I said, notoriety comes with a price, and Karen was caught up in it, big time. I presented these findings to my best friend, the defense attorney, who, it just so happened, had now taken the position of Supervisor in the Misdemeanor Division of the Prosecutor's Office, and was directly responsible for overseeing the filing of the charges against Karen. His response to me upon getting all of the information that would have immediately been cause to dismiss the charge was similar to the response of my other friend, the Captain; "There's nothing I can do."

Not only were the charges not dismissed, but the new State Attorney asked for a Special Prosecutor since Karen was an Assistant Public Defender, and the charges were increased as a result of her having children in the car. Of course, it became front-page news in the local rag of a newspaper, and for the next several months, Karen endured the courthouse rumor mill fodder by insignificant people who have very little concern for the truth, but are only concerned about "someone like Karen getting hers!" Her job was also in jeopardy since her boss, the compassionate and caring man he was, told her "if you are convicted, I will have to fire you."

No one really knew whether he would have or not, but at least he gave Karen the respect of "Innocent until Proven Guilty," the mantra of our judicial system and what his office existed upon. Since Karen had refused the Breathalyzer, she lost her license for ninety days, and during that period, her boss picked her up for work and brought her home almost every day. On days he couldn't, he would arrange for some other Assistant in the office to do so. He stood behind her throughout the whole event, and not once, gave a statement to the press regarding the incident or in any way negative towards Karen.

The details of the incident are not really that important, but Karen endured the humiliation of the arrest, the whispers in the courtroom by her adversaries and the embarrassment that was thrown upon her husband and her children for the next eleven months. She eventually got her license back and the record of the suspension removed after a judge overturned it based on a motion by her attorney and the fact that the sheriff's Department did not follow protocol. But in the meantime she had already done the ninety days without the license and taken all the required schools and paid all the administrative costs.

In October, 2003, in a two day trial, Karen Miller was found "Not Guilty" by a jury in less than twelve minutes of deliberation. The jury viewed the same video I did, reviewed the same documents I did, and reached the same conclusion I did; Karen Elizabeth Miller was not intoxicated, and that the arrest was the result of some other agenda on the part of the two deputies involved. I know this to be true since one of the jurors knew a friend of ours, after the fact, and told that person that they all could tell within an hour of the first day that something wasn't right. Then, when they viewed the video, heard the arresting officer testify, under oath, that Karen had passed all of the Field Sobriety Exercises but, he arrested her anyway, they couldn't wait to get into the deliberation stage and end this nightmare for Karen.

When It's Time

After the verdict was given, and as the arresting officer left the courtroom, I approached him. Although I was very angry and repulsed by what had taken place, I simply said to him, "I want to thank you for telling the truth in there when you could have very well lied, which wouldn't have helped, and in fact, would have made it worse for you seeing how the video was very revealing. I just hope that you remember that when you arrest someone, put the cuffs on them, and charge them with a crime, you change their lives forever, and the lives of their families. Please keep that in mind." While I understood that this officer, who had only been on the department for a short time, felt compelled to save face for his wife, who was also not that experienced, I also knew that what these two deputies did was the ultimate sin. They arrested, humiliated and tried to convict an innocent person based on personal agenda, not on facts.

In the span of just under twelve months, I realized what loyalty was, and I realized that the friends that are loyal in the good, and bad times, are few and far between. To this day, I have not spoken to the Captain and have only had casual "hellos" with the defense attorney, my best friend for over twenty years, and a Best Man at our wedding. Karen maintained a relationship with him as a result of her position, but it was strictly professional in nature. She always felt badly about the demise of our friendship and felt responsible. No matter how I tried to tell her that it was not her fault, she harbored that guilt in that long-lost gunny sack that I thought had been forgotten.

Of course the result of Karen being found not-guilty and exonerated was a small blurb in the paper, not the sensational headlines that preceded the trial and followed the arrest. Attorneys in the community, some who had stuck by her, and others who had been the source of much of the rumors, all patted her on the back and congratulated her. Once again, Karen was rising to the top in her notoriety and respect, and once again, we went about putting our lives back together and reenergizing our love and our family.

Karen quickly rose to the Supervisory level and was charged with making sure that the young attorneys just starting out in their careers were adjusting well and handling their cases. Although she appreciated the promotion, Karen was a trial lawyer and the courtroom was her dance floor. Her relationships with several of the older judges, the ones who had been on the bench for years, earned their positions and respected the law and the lawyers, was well founded. She would often go to lunch with several of the judges that she did not appear before and became interested in their families as much as they in hers. Although she had also been offered jobs at well established firms in the area, Karen always turned them down, and always cited her passion for being a Public Defender.

While everything seemed to be going fine on the outside, the brewing of past emotional events and the continual need for Karen to suppress those events eventually began to fester. For the next several years Karen would deal continuously with her alcohol abuse and necessity to deal with the bad things that had happened to her in her life in this manner. Our relationship became fractured on several occasions but never to the point of us parting. Karen did move out of our house for a period of about three months after several days of continuous drinking on her part, and total frustration on mine. During that three month period, however, we were together almost every day. She had rented a house about two miles away and closer to her job, and we maintained our marriage, and love, by battling through the issues. After it was all said and done our marriage was even stronger and our love even deeper. Karen went to a twelve-week counseling program that helped and she appeared back on track for recovery, albeit, temporarily.

During this time period, between the acquittal for the DUI arrest and the temporary separation, one thing had started to manifest itself more than I understood. Her supervisor, the one from the restaurant that I had cautioned Karen about, had now become Karen's best friend, both in and out of the office. They seemed inseparable at times, and the occasional Happy-Hour became the nightly routine.

When It's Time

It was not uncommon for Karen to leave the office with her supervisor in the middle of the afternoon then call me to come and pick one or both of them up from some bar or restaurant later in the evening because neither one could drive. Sometimes I would have to pick up Karen and sit there and wait with her friend until her husband, a man that was totally not involved in his marriage, would come and pick her up.

Many times I would have to go get Karen who had gone out with this supervisor, drive her home, and have someone take me back to get her car so she would have it to go to work in the morning. And, on more than one occasion, drive her supervisor home as well or at the very least have to follow her to her house over ten miles away. It was also not uncommon for me to come home in the mid-afternoon hours to find them both either drinking, or drunk, sitting around the pool. I would always question Karen about how they could get away with it and she would always say, "She's my supervisor, I'm with her." What Karen and I would both learn over the course of the next few years was that Karen appeared to be nothing but a pawn to this person and Karen was being used by this friend to cover up her own emotional dysfunctions and alcohol, and other, problems.

This became a tenuous situation between Karen and I and one that often was the center of discourse in our marriage. However, as much as I tried to convince Karen that this person was truly not her friend, but was just using her to satisfy her own emotional and addiction issues, Karen would always accuse me of trying to "control her" the way that Ray did. I don't know if she truly felt this way, or if it was just justification for her doing the things that she knew she had no control over. Whatever it was, Karen was being protected by the one person in the office that was just like her, also had the power to protect or destroy Karen, and most of all, use and abuse Karen for her own agenda.

I was not the only one that tried to warn Karen about this person. Other supervisors would also talk to Karen about her relationship, and on several occasions, call me to talk to me about it. I would tell them my concerns as well but that basically, I had no control over it.

Other attorneys in her office that had becomes friends with both of us would also try to intervene, but Karen had her mind set. Karen and her supervisor were best friends, and no one was going to make that change. Karen, above all, was a loyal friend, as she was a loyal wife and mother. But her loyalties toward her friend began to take priority over her loyalty for her family, and this led to a near disastrous ending for Karen and me.

In 2003 I was chosen for a four-month assignment in Italy to head up an investigative and inspections office there in coordination with our sister agency, Customs and Border Protection. The training involved two weeks in Miami and two weeks in D.C. During the training details, which were separated by only a couple of weeks in between, Karen became more and more attached to her new lifestyle with her best friend and less and less concerned about the family.

Her job, for the most part, was not in jeopardy since her best friend/supervisor covered for her and Karen was, by far, still one of the best attorneys in the office. On several nights Karen would call me while I was either in Miami or D.C., incoherent, emotionally distraught and displaying a total fear of abandonment from my absence. I would always assure her that I would be back but it seemed to have little effect. It had gotten so out of hand that I had actually contemplated cancelling the assignment to Italy, but then, Karen seemed to right the ship for the moment.

The plan was that I would go over to Italy in October, get settled, and then her and our son, along with my daughter and my oldest grandson would come over right after Thanksgiving. Then, Karen, her mother and our son and daughter would come over during the Christmas and New Year Holidays and I would return home in January. Things were going good leading up to my departure in October and I left as scheduled. What seemed to be going as planned, it turned out, was a fast ride downhill for Karen. Her best friend took every advantage of Karen being here by herself, without my "supervision" or "control" and it quickly turned into a party house at our home. I received a call from one of my neighbors who displayed great concern for what was going on at the house. I had several conversations about this with Karen and she assured me everything was alright and they were just having fun and attempting to handle Karen's separation anxieties.

When It's Time

As planned, Karen, my daughter, our son and my grandson arrived in Pisa, Italy right after Thanksgiving.

What was supposed to be a grand reunion for Karen and I, and an interesting and fun trip for my daughter and grandson, turned out to be pure hell for the seven days they were there. Karen got off the plane in a highly inebriated state, and stayed that way the entire time. As I put her back on the plane for their return trip home, I made it quite clear that things needed to change. I was assured they would. When Karen got back home, she had the support and encouragement of her best friend, who was quite comfortable at manipulating Karen and people like her, and the game was on yet again.

Just before Christmas, 2003, Karen, our children and her mother arrived for the two week visit. The first few days were great as we toured the Tuscany region, took a trip to Parma, getting lost in the mountain pass as the snow fell. The children played in the snow, the first time for either of them, while we all sat and stared at the map trying to figure out how the hell we were going to get back to the house I rented. Christmas was wonderful. I had managed to get a Christmas tree and lots of small gifts from the Army Base in Pisa that we had privileges at while on duty there. Everything was fine, then, for whatever reason, Karen totally lost control and began drinking to the extent that on New Year's Eve, she left with her mother and children to go to France for a few days.

I spent New Year's Eve and day, alone and afraid. Upon their return a day before they were to depart, Karen's mother informed me that Karen had begun having seizures and she was going to make her go to the doctor when they arrived home. For me, although not the last straw, it was getting pretty damn close. I cut my assignment short and flew out just before Karen and the rest did, arriving home about two hours before them.

After her arrival back home, Karen had more seizures and continued to drink and take prescription medicines. She was eventually admitted to the hospital and subsequently told that she needed to attend a rehab facility on the other side of the state. Karen did go, and the change in her in just a week was remarkable. For nearly six months after she left that facility, Karen was the perfect wife, mother, lover and attorney. Then, her associations with her best friend resumed.

While Karen was at the facility for her rehab, not once did her best friend visit, call, ask about her or even attempt to show concern. This may be due to the fact that while Karen was in Italy for the Christmas period, apparently my house was utilized for much "socializing" and "entertaining" by her friend as possible. This was told to me by a neighbor who knew Karen's friend/supervisor. The final stroke to me, and one that still irritates me and makes my skin crawl to this day, is that when I returned home, just before Karen, to my house that had been vacant for nearly two weeks, I was greeted by this awful pungent smell as I entered.

I discovered in the master bath, someone had vomited in the large tub and left it while Karen was in Italy with me. There was so much vomit, mostly red in color, resembling red wine, which Karen detested, that it had been infested with maggots. It took me nearly three days to get the smell out and several scrubbing ventures to remove the stains. Although I don't know for sure, in my mind, there was only one person that could possibly have done that, and, for me, enough was enough.

But, as much as I continued to caution Karen about her association with this individual, she continued to tell me that I was trying to control her. And, besides, Karen would always say, "She's also my boss, I have a career to think of, and I don't want to piss her off." I, again, wasn't the only one concerned about Karen's association with this person. Another friend of Karen's, a prosecutor, had also warned Karen repeatedly about this so called "best friend," and I remember her telling Karen, "Not only will she throw you under the bus given the need, but she will back it up and run over you again." This warning fell on deaf ears to Karen, mainly because this prosecutor had the same emotional and addiction problems as Karen, so Karen felt that maybe this other person was jealous. As it would also come to fruition down the road, at a time when Karen needed this other friend the most, she too would show disloyalty and hurt Karen so very deeply in the end.

When It's Time

Karen was getting quite the reputation, and not the good kind, along with her friend, and as is usually the case, reputations tend to stay with you for a long time, in spite of the facts surrounding situations one might find one's self in. And for Karen, the reputation would be one that would eventually cause her great hardship and another bout in the "Dirty Laundry" arena. The best friend seemed to be Teflon coated and always managed to skate from the accusations and insinuations. She often feigned concern for Karen and would appear to be the one person that was there for Karen, however, everyone knew the truth. But since Karen was relatively new to the area and the office, she always seemed to take the brunt of the downfalls. Oh, and her best friend, would learn very well how to drive "the bus."

CHAPTER THIRTEEN - DANCE WITH THE DEVIL

From 2005 to 2007, things did get somewhat under control. Karen was hanging out less and less with her friend, but did maintain a close personal relationship. Our marriage, once again, seemed to be growing stronger. Our son had entered high school and was doing well on the football and track team. Everyone seemed to settle into the normal routine of being a family. We bought a small house across from a lake in a town seventy eight miles from us and spent many weekends there enjoying the boat we also purchased. We took our first cross country motorcycle trip to California with another couple, Mike and Libby that would become a ritual for the next eight years. When it came to travelling on the motorcycle, Karen was very much at home and enjoyed the many stops under the overpasses to sit out torrential storms, or ducking into the nearest gas station to get out of the hail storms. Since it was my idea to do this, I was also charged with planning the first trip. We went from our driveway to California, up through Oregon, the Dakotas and back down through Tennessee and home again; eight thousand miles. While everyone enjoyed the trip and we had a lot of fun, I was never allowed to plan the trip lengths again. It seems that I may have overdone the calculations on the first trip.

On each and every one of our trips, sometimes during the course of the journey, one of us would always get mad at another, except Mike and Karen. While Libby and I were quite serious about things, Mike and Karen had a lackadaisical attitude that brought them close together as friends. Sharing the same birthday didn't hurt. Every year the four of us would try to celebrate their birthdays together and Karen felt very at ease with Mike and Libby, both at home, and on our trips.

Over the next six years we went to South Dakota and Wyoming twice, Colorado twice, upstate New York where we rented a cabin in the middle of nowhere, the Carolinas and Tennessee. Every trip was a blast and, for as long as we were on the motorcycle, Karen exhibited no stress, worries or the need to drink or take medicine.

Those trips were truly the type that memories were made of and ones that I have cherished. After every trip Karen would make a collage of the places we were and hang them on our wall, where they still are today.

Karen was also charged with plotting our courses and each year before each trip I had to secure the maps of all the states we were going to visit and take rides in. She was marvelous at getting us on the right roads, away from interstates, that made the trips most enjoyable. When it came to this task, Karen was the best, and even Mike's GPS couldn't compete with her. While she could navigate across country with ease, she often had a hard time navigating around the town and adjoining cities where we live. She also was not a very good driver, especially backing up. One night she got really mad at me over something insignificant, stormed to her car, and took off down the street. I came out to the front yard to try to apologize and as she got about two houses away she stopped, put the vehicle in reverse and starting backing up a little too fast. She ran over our neighbor's mailbox, took it out completely, without putting a scratch on her new BMW. The next morning, as I was drinking my coffee looking out the front window, I saw the neighbor out there with a post-hole digger and a new mailbox. I walked outside and all he said to me was, "Damn kids." As I nearly choked on my coffee, I went inside and told Karen she probably should not go outside just yet as Mark was putting his mailbox back up. It wasn't until several years later I told him the truth. Given the circumstances, he laughed and thought it was a good memory.

I had also bought Karen her very own "Muscle Car." Right before my divorce from my previous wife I had just completed the restoration of a 1969 Dodge Charger. I pulled it out of a field in Tennessee and spent four years restoring it. I sold it after the divorce but always wanted to "build" another one. I told Karen I was looking for something to buy that needed to be restored and she suggested an AMX, since she had one in college. Not knowing what the hell an AMX was, I did some research and just so happened to find out my nephew in California had several so I bought the one that needed the most work.

When It's Time

I remember rolling it off the truck that delivered it and Karen saying, "That's nice, but good luck." It indeed did need a lot of work and for the next five years I went about restoring it to pristine condition. It was Karen's car, and she loved driving it and taking it to car shows. It wasn't until 2013 that she won her first trophy and was so proud she called everyone she knew.

Karen was doing well, our marriage and family were strong once again, and life, for the moment, appeared to be going our way for a change. Karen was a different person, and, at last, she seemed totally at peace without any need to think about her job, her problems, and least of all, her past. Things would start to change once again in 2008.

On December 28, 2007, one day after Karen's birthday, Karen's boss, the man who stood by Karen's side during her DUI arrest, passed away suddenly at the age of 62. While the entire office and the community were saddened, Karen took the loss very hard. She had grown very close to this man and he always had a friendly word of encouragement for Karen, no matter what the issue. This left a void in the office which meant that an interim Public Defender would have to be appointed. The appointment went to Karen's best friend, and supervisor and it appeared that maybe, just maybe, Karen's loyalty to this person would work out to her benefit. There was a catch to the appointment, however. Since the position wasn't up for reelection for three more years, a special election was to be held within six months. Whoever won the election would then have to run for the office again in three years. Karen's supervisor went into full election mode and Karen, being the kind of friend and loyal supporter she was, quickly jumped on board, even though two other people that Karen had become friends with were also running for the office.

It became a very stressful time in our relationship. If her friend had lost the election, which was only seven months or so away, it was a good bet that she would have been terminated by the new Public Defender, and Karen, in all likelihood, might have been also, although the other two candidates also respected Karen for her ability and knew the position she was put in by her best friend.

While her best friend, now candidate, demanded loyalty from those around her, she often times wasn't much for returning that demand, and had a reputation of being less than understanding to those she supervised, another quality that Karen had seen firsthand and I had pointed out to her over the course of the past several years.

Nonetheless, Karen went full bore in helping her friend win the election, even to the point of offering to end her own career should one of the other candidates win. As Karen told her friend, who admittedly was not half the attorney that Karen was and had handled very few cases over the past five years; "We will go open an office together and I'll handle the clients and you handle the administrative stuff until you are comfortable. Don't worry, I'll teach you everything you need to know." To Karen, that was what being a best friend was about, and she, under no circumstances, was going to be disloyal.

Karen attended every political function to be at the side of her friend. She would take personal time off to stand on the corners of major intersections holding signs at rush hour in the heat of the Florida sun. And, not only did she raise a large amount of money for her friend's campaign from all of her family and friends, she had myself and Snake going to three different counties putting up large billboard signs, sometimes up to our knees in water and other times in the driving rain or boiling sun. Although I really wanted no part of all of this, given my opinion and history with the friend, I told Karen, "I am doing this for you and you alone. I love you and I want you to be happy. This is not for her, it is for you."

One part of me wanted her friend to win because I knew what it would mean for Karen's career, or at least I believed I knew. Another part of me wanted her to lose because then maybe Karen would see the reality of what her friend was. I don't know if Karen would have foregone her career as a public defender, a career she loved, had her friend lost, but as it turned out, it was a question that remained unanswered. Her friend won the special election easily and things around the office changed, and changed rapidly.

Karen was eventually promoted to the position of Deputy Assistant and handled several of the felony tracts in the office. Her career, it seemed, was quickly elevating and her reputation as a supervisor was one that was well received. Her relationship with her best friend, now the person in charge, however, diminished rapidly.

When It's Time

As politicians go, her best friend had quickly learned the intricate secrets of how to survive, knowing full well that within two years, she would have to run for the office again. Those that had been loyal to her during the special election were left untouched. However, those that were not quickly found themselves out of jobs or relocated to different positions. Since the office covered five counties, some of the more experienced and better attorneys that fell into disfavor were sent packing to some remote county that involved a long commute on a daily basis. Karen, however, for the most part, seemed secure, but even she began to see the dramatic changes in the office and started to feel uncomfortable with them. Karen, although receiving the promotion she wanted, also started to feel ostracized by her best friend who had taken over the office. The lunches were gone, the afternoon chats were a thing of the past and she felt her friendship gradually dwindle to one of a professional, not personal, relationship. Karen tried to keep in touch with the courtroom as much as she could but also be the supervisor that she was expected to be. As reputations go, Karen was one of the finest attorneys in town and had a caring and compassionate sense about her. It was very hard for her to say "no" to anyone that asked for a favor. And this inability to say no was the beginning of her dramatic fall from grace.

In May, 2009, Karen was asked by another attorney in the office to help him in a trial. The other attorney, a friend of Karen's, one whom she had mentored and socialized with, was getting ready to do a trial for an individual charged with numerous counts that would result in a prison sentence if convicted. Although this attorney was experienced, he lacked the motivation, and quite frankly the skills, to undertake such a trial on his own, so he asked Karen to assist him. On the day of jury selection, Karen had gotten up to go to court but wasn't feeling well. At first we thought it was just a flu virus or something to that effect, but she felt very uneasy and wasn't sure what was wrong. I asked her to stay home but she insisted on going to court to help the other attorney knowing full well he could not have handled the beginning phase by himself. I refused to let her drive and took her to court. I dropped her at the front doors of the courthouse thirty minutes before she was to be in court. She did look a bit uneasy but assured me she was fine.

Later, in the early afternoon, Karen was driven home by another person in the office. She came in, appearing worried and confused. I had no idea what had happened and Karen was being very secretive about it. That evening, I got a call from a friend asking me if I had seen the news. Karen, it said, was accused of being drunk in court and a mistrial was granted. The attorney she was helping panicked at the prospect of having to do the trial by himself and instead of asking for a recess due to Karen's illness, he asked the judge for a mistrial, which was granted.

The next day it was on the front page of the local newspaper, right there, complete with the statement her best friend, the boss, had given. The benefit of the doubt was not provided to Karen by her boss, in spite of the fact there was no proof that what was alleged actually happened. The statement pretty much said that Karen Miller had been "suspended from the office and an internal investigation was being completed."

The internal investigation, it seemed, was no more than a subject from the office asking everyone involved if Karen had been drinking prior to going to court. It also never included asking me, the one person that was with Karen the entire night before and drove her to work that morning. Internal investigations have a way of finding what you want them to find, and Karen, it seemed, was "guilty without being innocent," nor would she ever be innocent. The chips were starting to fall, it appeared, since Karen was probably the "one" person in the office who knew the most about her friend, and not all of it was good. Karen knew "where the bodies were buried," to use an old cliché.

During the investigation, the client, who sat next to Karen, the other attorney, and even the judge on the bench said that they did not "smell" anything that would indicate Karen's being drunk. They all said the same thing, Karen just looked ill. Of course, none of this made it to the paper, or even in the internal report. Karen was immediately suspended, and was told that in order for her to return to work, she would have to go to counseling with a doctor approved by the office and engage in a performance contract that basically contained an admission of her guilt and being put on a probationary period for as long as "the boss" deemed necessary as well as being immediately demoted, which would have a major impact on her career and retirement.

When It's Time

For nearly a month, Karen was not allowed to return to work while the office looked for ways to terminate her. Both Karen and I knew the truth, and Karen knew that something was wrong physically so she went to her personal physician for tests. She was then referred to an endocrinologist who diagnosed Karen with the onset of Type II Diabetes, which, if unknown or treated, results in low blood sugar incidents known as hypoglycemia.

The symptoms of hypoglycemia can be very similar to being intoxicated, including giving off a sweet fruity smell, and can render a person incoherent and confused. Not only did Karen's personal physician and endocrinologist verify this diagnosis, but also the doctor that her new boss made her see as well. In spite of this revelation, her best friend, the boss, was intent on getting rid of Karen and refused to accept any of these medical opinions. The contract for performance evaluation and counseling stood, and Karen was sent to another division, in another city, working for the one person Karen despised in the office.

This person was the epitome of incompetence and arrogance, and had been put in her position after the election because she had been a "long-time" friend of the boss, but on a casual basis, not the kind of relationship Karen had had with the boss. This other person was pretty much disrespected by anyone that worked for her as a result of her incompetence, but more so for the fact that she treated everyone like dirt and had exclusive rights on "kissing ass" to get ahead.

Karen eventually signed the contract, with some minor adjustments, and returned to work. At the same time Karen filed a complaint with the Equal Employment Opportunity Commission, (EEOC) since a person with an illness such as diabetes is protected under the Americans with Disability Act and the EEOC handles these complaints. Based on the diagnosis from three doctors, the statements of the witnesses, and myself in the complaint, the EEOC accepted the complaint and notified the boss. This, of course, did not go over well, and, regardless of what her personal feelings were, the boss had to answer the complaint. During the process Karen was basically "per sona non grata" and had set herself up for retribution to come.

In the complaint filed by Karen against her new boss, and former best friend, Karen substantiated what everyone else also knew was true. Part of the complaint affidavit included the following statement from Karen:

"After she was elected and appointed me supervisor, her demeanor changed. Any expression or discussion by a supervisor was shot down with a black mark on your record for disagreeing. She drove away experienced lawyers by threatening them with employment contracts or being fired. Virtually all of these people were over 50. …..Since I could not drink as a result of the diabetic incident, I was out, my supervisory duties were taken away and I was banished to no man's land, demoted with a cut in pay and complete humiliation. Young attorneys would secretly ask me for advice because they were afraid to be seen speaking with me. Once I was no longer able to drink with her or have long lunches of booze, I was out."

It became apparent to Karen that this was retribution since, as also noted in her complaint; "Two other attorneys and the Human Resources Director had all been convicted of DUI offenses and retained their positions."

The complaint was settled through mediation and Karen received her back annual and sick leave that she had been forced to use while suspended, and also received her salary back. Her demotion, however, stood, since her position had immediately been filled upon her suspension by a much younger and much less experienced attorney that now spent all of her time with the boss, including the "long lunches."

While it was a victory for Karen, some victories are just precursors to losing the battle in the long run, and Karen had now made an enemy of a person who, at one time, was her best friend, and who Karen had offered to end her own career for. Vindictive, hateful people like her friend, do not forget very easily. The entire process was time consuming and emotionally destructive for Karen. The "best friend" necessity that Karen always wanted, had again, been destroyed. It of course never made it into the news, nor did her boss ever apologize for Karen's treatment. Her relationship with a person that had once been her friend both in and out of the office was now deteriorated to a point of no return.

CHAPTER FOURTEEN - YOUR REPUTATION PRECEDES YOU

Over the next fourteen moths, Karen and I enjoyed our life together, spending many weekends at the lake where Karen learned to water ski. She also took great pride in teaching our now teen-aged son to ski as well, with, of course, some guidance from me. In the summer of 2009 we took our annual motorcycle trip, this time to North Carolina and the Blue Ridge area. We rode the "Tail of the Dragon," toured all of the Blue Ridge Parkway and for a while, Karen managed, again, to put the past few months behind her. Christmas that year was probably one of the most beautiful times we had ever had together. In 2010 we travelled to Wyoming and South Dakota and visited Yellowstone and Mt. Rushmore, stopping on the way home to visit the property we had bought in Tennessee in the hopes of someday building a house, there, complete with horses and a large garden. Karen loved horses and was an avid rider in her youth. All Karen ever wanted was to sit in the window of our house on the hill overlooking our property, writing her novel, while watching me plow the garden that I would be tasked to create. This dream was what kept her battling her demons for many years.

The events of the past year had been buried deep inside Karen's psyche, but just not deep enough. Over this period of time Karen battled with depression and, for the most part, kept it under control. Her relationship with her former best friend was at the low end of casual, and Karen secretly put on a happy face each and every day and went about being what she was, the best public defender in the office. She won numerous trials and had a record of success that was matched by none. This was not only as a result of her abilities as an attorney, but also a result of her genuine compassion for her clients and her being comfortably at home in the trial process.

Her reputation amongst her peers, both in and out of the office, was one of admiration and respect, and she was again offered numerous jobs with private attorneys in the area. She never accepted any of these jobs since her passion was to be a public defender, and she had dedicated her life to that passion. There were occasional bouts with alcohol, but they were few and far between. To Karen, however, they were still too many and something that she desperately wanted to conquer once and for all.

The most difficult part about conquering demons such as an addictive personality is having the support of those around you. While Karen had the support of her family, most of all me, she never received the support she needed from friends, or at least those she believed were her friends. Karen had always been known as a "party girl" and the friends and associations she continued to keep preyed heavily on that reputation. Misery does indeed love company, and the need for Karen to have friends far outweighed the need for Karen to remain under control and free from her addictions. She tripped up along the way a few times, but never to the extent that it affected her work. Eventually, Karen finally realized that the company she was keeping was nothing more than shallow acquaintances and that she needed to change for good. Karen learned of a facility in Seattle that utilized a 10-day inpatient program combining medically-supervised counter-conditioning therapy, counseling and group therapy. She decided to go and try to get herself back on tract and overcome her addiction forever.

The change in Karen that took place was very positive. She was a completely different person after her trip to Seattle, and for once, it seemed, she had figured it out. The problems with programs like this however, or any program for that matter is, unless you address the underlying fears and depression that leads to the addictions, you are just touching the tip of the situation. But, all in all, Karen was doing fine with her treatment success. However, she forgot to continue to address the medical issue, that being the diabetes.

Karen would have occasional bouts of hypoglycemia as a result of not eating properly more than anything else. When she quit drinking, she gained weight. To counter this, Karen went on the proverbial diet, and not the healthy kind; she just quit eating. She monitored her blood-sugar routinely at first upon receiving the diagnosis, but more times than not would forget to take the medication for the diabetes or just outright refused to take it, blaming it for her weight gains.

Being around Karen as long as I have been, I knew her idiosyncrasies and her emotional states. I knew when she had not eaten enough and suffered from low blood-sugar. I also knew when she had been drinking, which was not often during this time, or was just depressed as a result of something that happened at the office or some past event creeping into her mind just to screw with her.

The one thing that continued to give her the greatest emotional distress was the fact that her best friend had "stabbed" her in the back the way she did, and that she had to go to work each day under the supervision of a person that Karen despised as an attorney and a person. And, it seemed, this supervisor had been given the sole task of providing as much discomfort for Karen as she possibly could, within the realm of legality considering the EEOC incident of course. The more that Karen had to go to the office across the river in the adjoining city, and the more she had to work for this person, the more she began to become irritated and aggravated. But, also, the more she began to once again question the fairness of life and how "someone could be mean just for the sake of being mean."

August 12, 2010. It was a beautiful summer day, a Thursday to be exact. Karen and I had just passed our ninth Anniversary, a milestone that Karen was very proud of. She had never been with any person in a relationship as long as she had with me, and the struggles we went through seemed distant and faint in the memories. Karen had once told me she didn't know why I stayed with her and said, "I'm so afraid that you'll leave me if I get better since you won't have anyone to take care of, and you need someone to "fix" all the time."

I am not sure if she really felt that way or if it was an opportunity for confirmation of "my" loyalty. I simply told Karen, "I will never leave you. I will never abandon you, and I mean that. You don't need to get better on your own, you just need to realize that you have a man who loves you more than anything, and we can get through anything."

She smiled that beautiful smile that she always had when she was slightly sad yet hopeful. Karen could never understand why I stood by her with all her "problems" and how I couldn't realize that I would be so much better off without her. We often had discussions about this and the whole loyalty thing from a man seemed foreign to her. Sometimes, as we would lie in bed together and Karen would drift off to sleep, I would sit motionless just staring at her and how awesome she was. When she realized I was doing this, she would always smile, not needing to say anything, and, at those times, I believe she understood how much she meant to me. And Karen's loyalty to me was never ending as well. Karen was good at being loyal, but in her life's experiences, loyalty was a luxury that was not bestowed upon her regularly.

Karen often believed that she did not deserve love and this belief was very hard to break through. To me, and what I explained to her, "the problems, the trials and tribulations, are what makes our love so strong, and what gives me the opportunity to be the man you deserve, and also, what makes me love you so much more. If love is easy, it is often ignored. When it's hard, it makes you work harder at it, and the rewards are so much sweeter when you succeed. I love you for who you are, not what you do. I will always be there for you. I will always love you."

While Karen tried desperately to believe me, she found the reality of my love hard to grasp. Karen, it seemed, would always be affected by the past and it carried her into her present, and subsequently her future.

When It's Time

The night before August 12, 2010, Karen came home after work like any other night. She had a doctor's appointment the next day to have a problem with her foot examined. It was at a doctor's office in the city she now worked in, and a place she had never been before. While Karen was quite capable of navigating a six thousand mile trip across the country in any direction and back, using just a map from AAA, and could find her away around any major city in the United States given a bus route and time schedule, she had the most difficult time getting around in our own town, and especially in the city across the river that she very rarely went to.

She knew the way to the office and back from our home so going to a new doctor's office there, was somewhat of a challenge. She came home a little late that night explaining to me that she had been in her boss's office with the current supervisor telling her that she would not be in in the morning and was going to this new doctor. She said she was not going to file a leave slip until she got back to the office after the appointment because, since she was a new patient, she didn't know how long it would take. The meeting was very short and concise.

Before she went to bed Karen got on the computer to do a mapquest search to find the location of the doctor's office and the best way to get there. Her appointment was at 10:00am, so she wanted to leave early to find the office. Karen and I had our usual Wednesday night together with the children watching the one or two sitcoms we viewed as a family and retired rather early for bed.

The next morning, Karen brought me a cup of coffee, as she often did when she got up before me, took a shower and got dressed in a pair of blue jeans, T-shirt and flip-flops. She didn't want to wear shoes to the doctor's appointment since she was going there for a problem with her foot to begin with, but planned on coming home after the appointment to change once it was over. I was sitting at the dining room table reading the paper and drinking coffee when Karen left, telling me she would be back in a couple of hours. Everything was as it should be, normal as every day before recently, but this day would turn out so much differently.

Rickie D. Maness

Karen left the house at about 8:45am, after having her usual latte' and rushing out. Her appointment was at 9:45 and she didn't want to be late since she had to fill out paperwork that all new patients are required to do. And, she wasn't real sure where the doctor's office was. As I was sitting at the table, at 9:20am, my cell phone rang and it was Karen. I could sense something was wrong and she started talking rapidly telling me she had been involved in an accident and couldn't find the insurance card. I told her where it was in her car and she tried to explain to me where she was but that she was okay. She told me the sheriff's office had come and asked her to move her vehicle out of the roadway into a parking lot but she wasn't sure where she was. She said she would call me back. I started to get dressed when she called back, again, in a panic and said, "The sheriff's deputies are here and apparently I am going to be arrested." I asked what she was being arrested for and she replied, "I guess for not having my insurance card." I asked her again if she was alright, she said yes, but didn't know what was going on. I then heard one of the deputies say to her, "you need to get off the phone now, and get out of your car."

Karen told the officer she was on the phone with her husband and was trying to explain where she was and that I was on my way there. Again, the deputy said, "you need to get out of your car now and hang up the phone." The deputies knew Karen, knew where she worked, and also knew that I was a former law enforcement officer. None of that meant anything in the big scheme of things, or, it meant everything. Karen was arrested for DUI, at 9:30 in the morning, going to a doctor's appointment.

The deputies searched the vehicle, found no evidence of any alcohol or drugs, but arrested her because she was sitting in her car, sweating, in August, and seemed to be confused and disoriented, after just being involved in a traffic accident, an accident where she ran into the rear of the vehicle in front of her causing her vehicle to be inoperable. The only thing found in the vehicle was an alternate pair of shoes, some clothes, a half of cup of coffee and half of a bagel, as well as the receipt from when she had just purchased the coffee and bagel ten minutes earlier from the Panera Bread restaurant two miles away.

When It's Time

Karen exhibited all the symptoms of a hypoglycemic event, became confused as to where she was, and while trying to get back to the highway to go to the doctor's office, ran into the vehicle stopped in front of her. Research will show that police often mistake events such as these with a person being under the influence.

The original officer on the scene was a volunteer and felt that Karen was alright to drive her vehicle through a major intersection of over six lanes, make a U-turn, and pull into the parking lot next to the Wendy's. The second officer to arrive was a traffic investigator who, upon recognizing Karen, immediately called another deputy, one that Karen had just had a case against, knew very well, and was married to a prosecutor. Before any field sobriety test was done, and before anything was investigated, Karen was told she was going to be arrested. She was then placed under arrest and taken into custody.

Before Karen arrived at the jail, it was all over the courthouse, in particular the prosecutor's office, and had filtered down to her boss, her former best friend. When I made it to the scene they were just taking her car away on the wrecker and the deputy refused to tell me anything other than Karen was arrested. In fact, he was downright smug, smirked, and exhibited an arrogance that I, in my professional career, would have greatly been ashamed of. It was very apparent to me what had just happened.

Karen got released from jail later that afternoon and was absolutely beside herself, assuring me that she had not been drinking or taking any medication. Having talked to her on the phone during the incident, and witnessing her leaving that morning, as well as what I had observed at the accident scene, she didn't have to explain anything to me. She was humiliated, embarrassed, hurt and could not figure out, again, why someone would do this, in her mind, just because they could, and just to be mean.

That evening, Karen received a call from the supervisor saying that the boss, her friend, wanted to meet with her tomorrow at 10:00am, in the office of the supervisor, in the city across the river. There was no concern, regard or genuine compassion for what Karen had just been through.

The next morning, the local news crew came to the door, complete with camera and reporter, attempting to get "the scoop." I, as politely as I could, told them to leave and not come back, that Karen had nothing to say. The headline on the 12:00 noon edition was, of course, "Karen Miller, Assistant Public Defender, arrested again."

When we arrived at the supervisor's office the next day, both Karen and I went in together. As we came into the office, the boss, Karen's former best friend, and the supervisor, the henchwoman, were sitting at the desk. In a situation like this, a lot of things can be said to soften the blow. But, in spite of what you intend on doing, the first thing that should be broached is concern, compassion, and the opportunity for an explanation. None of that was displayed by Karen's former best friend. The only words that were said to Karen were, "This is your termination letter. I need your keys to the office and your identification badge." As Karen placed her keys and identification on the desk, took the letter from her boss, she simply looked at her former friend and said, "You could have told me that on the phone," and then we left.

It was now apparent this person had completely evolved into a person with no compassion or concern and had exacted her vindictiveness. She didn't care about Karen, wanted no explanation, only wanted what Karen felt was her revenge, and this, to her, was it. Funny how people like that get to make up the rules, ruin people's lives and seem to always get away with it. But, in the end, their judgment will be held, and they will have to explain their actions to the only one that matters, and that, I have on good sources.

The words to describe the betrayal that Karen went though as a result of this episode are not definable in any language. Once again, Karen had been the victim of being a compassionate, caring and loving person, who would not hurt anyone. And once again, fate had stepped in to deal Karen another blow to her emotional being. Karen never really got over the events that her former friend put into motion for no apparent reason other than pure vengeance.

When It's Time

It took nearly two months before Karen could recover from this hurt and pain, and this hurt and pain would be the beginning of the ultimate end. To say that Karen was "smitten" by bad luck would be a simple justification. While Karen sometimes placed herself in positions to be a target, she also never really understood that there are just evil people in this world, and the profession she had chosen as her lifelong passion was full of such people. And, mix in politics and shallow, spiteful and disingenuous people like her former friend, disastrous results will abound.

While Karen always wanted to be "the big fish in the little pond"; she never understood that the bigger you are, the more people want to take you down. Karen was good at what she did, and she did it with passion for the underdog. That is something that people in this day and age, just don't have, especially the person that Karen had once trusted to be her friend, and the one person that was perhaps more responsible for the upcoming events than any person alive.

As for me, I knew that the career and profession I had dedicated my life to had changed to the point that I didn't even recognize it any more. The badge became a weapon, not a calling, and people like the individuals that arrested Karen that day on August 12th, 2010, were the epitome of what I never believed would be. So, Karen and I, once again, went about trying to put her life together again and our lives back together, since she was me, and I her. This time, however, it was personal for me, and my love for her became never ending and the crux of my being. While I truly felt in my heart that Karen was set up, and was a target of small insignificant people with nothing to add to society except their own version of justice, especially the two officers involved, we would, as it happened, never find out.

Karen's boss and former best friend refused to talk to Karen, what was done was done. Karen did reach out for her several times, and she did return Karen's call once accusing Karen of being drunk when she left the voicemail, which certainly was not the case. The absolute lack of compassion for a woman who had just had her life, once again, ripped out from under her, was astonishing.

The press, of course, ran a story for three days, intermittently. The video taken at the jail showed in abundant fashion, Karen fully stable, upright and in control, even when the arresting officer made her walk backwards, handcuffed behind her back, to a chair across the room. I couldn't tell if he had an obvious smirk on his face, maybe it was my imagination, but one thing I have learned over the years is "karma" truly is a bitch, and it will eventually bite, maybe not in the time-frame you would like to see it come around, but eventually, it does catch up to you. And, I certainly hope that this man receives all the karma that is deserved of one who was vengeful and spiteful and in a position of authority to exercise that vengeance. People like that should never be given the power to enact the law.

CHAPTER FIFTEEN - WHAT NOW?

The next few weeks for Karen were the toughest I have ever had to witness her go through. She had once again been targeted for what appeared to be revenge by a person in a position of power. She had her former best friend humiliate her, both personally, and professionally. She had no job, no career, and truthfully, I became very worried. Since she had not been convicted of anything, the Florida Bar did not get involved, as of yet. That was still to come, however, and it would again be the result of perceived vengeance by another person in power and for the mere sake of being mean. Karen struggled every day to get out of bed, and on many days she didn't. The press eventually gave up on the story since there was little else to report at this time. They had completed their laundry list and moved on to whomever else they could destroy. I began to become intensely worried about Karen's emotional stability and we spent a few days at the lake house to try and get past, not over, what had just occurred. Despite all of my efforts, Karen sank deeper and deeper into depression. Now I began to be gravely concerned.

Then, out of the blue, Karen received a call from an attorney that she casually knew, covered cases in court for him, and had earned his respect as a lawyer. He owned his own building, had a small practice, and was retiring. He offered Karen the opportunity to move into his building, open her office, finish the few cases he had, and get her life back together, all the while rent-free until she got set up. Suddenly, the spark in Karen's eyes started to reappear and she felt that maybe, just maybe, life had dealt her a good hand.

I remember the first day that I went to look at the office that was offered to her. Donald, the attorney that made the offer was there. He was a person that I had known for over thirty years, and although somewhat an eccentric man, he was compassionate and caring. We had known each other since I was with the sheriff's department and, although I never had a case against him he and I would always talk overlooking the balcony of the second floor of the courthouse. It was quietly known as "his office" by every attorney in town since he would sit there for hours almost every day.

As I walked in, he greeted me. "Thank you for giving Karen this chance" I said to him. His words resonated in me as he responded, "I've been where she is before. I've had to defend myself as well. I am giving her this chance because, quite frankly, she is one of the best defense attorney's in town, bar none. I think what happened is not right and I want her to get back on her feet. She's a good person who got hooked up with the wrong people."

Donald apparently had his own ideas about Karen's former boss, and also did not have much respect for the local law enforcement. Donald and I came from the old school of thinking; you did what was right, everyone knew the rules and the lines, and you didn't cross them, on either side. All of that had changed over the past decade and he, as I, was very disgusted by the antics of some police officers and attorneys in town. He wasn't real fond of many of the judges either as they all seemed to believe that the "Bench" was their birthright, and that lawyers, not them of course, were stupid and ignorant. That was why he was retiring, he had had enough. There's an old saying; "those who can do and those who can't teach." That applied to most of the judges in this town. They were either incapable of making it as an attorney, their family had money, or they were former politicians who felt the need to continue on the public dole by being appointed judges. Most of the appointments that were made by the Governor when a vacancy came open fell into the latter. The appreciation towards this man for giving Karen the opportunity to bring herself out of the pits can never be bestowed abundantly.

Karen and I spent the next several weeks setting up her office, buying furniture, and going about getting her new career started. Immediately she began getting clients, mostly former clients she had while a public defender, and even some who were clients of the public defender's office who heard she was in her own office and contacted her. Karen knew that she was very capable and much respected, and things started to take off. She hired a secretary, Cynthia, part-time at first, which eventually evolved into a full-time position.

When It's Time

Cynthia had been a former client of Karen's while she was at the public defender's office. Karen didn't like her much at first, thought she was brash and a bit too "street wise." She was younger than Karen, but not much. She was a Black female that had never had a job, only a high school education, and had been living the past several years getting public assistance.

Jobs for people like Cynthia were few and far between in this town, and Karen, of all people, knew this. After Karen had Cynthia's case dismissed, they became friends. When Karen opened her office, she called Cynthia and offered her a job, agreeing to teach Cynthia all there was to know about being a legal Secretary. As it also turned out, both Cynthia and Karen had the same birthday, and Cynthia had gone through much of what Karen had gone through. They were good for each other at the moment.

Cynthia, not having a reliable car to drive, would often not be able to get to the office on time and would have to use Karen's car to go to the courthouse to file papers. Karen rectified this by buying Cynthia a car. The look on her face, and the tears she displayed when Karen called her to meet her at the office on a Saturday to "get some paperwork done" and Cynthia came into the driveway and saw Karen and I standing there with the keys in Karen's hand, was worth a thousand hugs. To Cynthia, no one had ever done anything like this for her, to Karen; it was what she was and couldn't understand why no one had ever done anything like this for Cynthia before. A short time after that, Cynthia came into the office and with a giant smile, told Karen that for the first time in a long time, she was no longer accepting public assistance. Cynthia was so proud as a person, and Karen was so proud that she had been given the opportunity to help her. But, then again, that was Karen Elizabeth Miller.

For the next year, things seemed to be going great. Karen was still struggling with depression now and again, but had curtailed the alcohol to a few drinks a week. Our life, it seemed, was finally going to where we both had wanted it. Then, Karen took on a client that, ultimately, would be the worst decision of her life.

This client was an elderly man that had been involved in a homicide thirty years prior and had been on the run for all that time. He had assumed a new identity and was finally caught when he went to renew his license in California. He was arrested, charged with second degree murder, and brought back for trial. Karen had represented him while at the public defender's office when the case was in the infancy stage. When Karen was terminated his case was assigned to the supervisor of the division, the one Karen despised. A few months after Karen had opened her office she was contacted, through another attorney, by this man. He had developed a relationship with Karen for the couple of weeks she had his case and did not like the new public defender that was assigned when Karen was fired. He felt that she "was more interested in obtaining a plea rather than trying his case." Karen agreed to take the case knowing that he had very little money, but to her, it was a chance to get vindication.

Throughout the early months of 2011 Karen prepared for this case and took it to trial. Most of the witnesses had died or relocated to other states. All of the officers involved had retired and at best, the state had a medium chance of winning. Karen realized that the state's only witness could be easily discredited and prepared the defense around this fact. Then, just prior to the start of the trial, the prosecutor, a woman that Karen knew but had very little respect for in an adversarial venue, informed Karen that they were not going to use the "main" witness, and the trial began. On the first day of the trial the prosecution called the witness that they had advised Karen they weren't going to use. Karen immediately asked for a recess to give her the chance to depose this witness for the sake of discrediting her. The judge in the case, who was getting set to retire after this trial, another former prosecutor, denied Karen's request and the state moved forward.

Stress can cause a lot of problems for someone, especially when it also involves someone with diabetes. Karen spent hours upon hours, into the late night, trying to figure out how to discredit the state's case, knowing that she could not bring anything about the main witness at this time since she did not have "official records."

When It's Time

Evidence is only admitted when it is verified and accountable to the facts. She was doing a good job of it until in the middle of the second day the prosecutor approached the bench and told the judge she thought "Ms. Miller was under the influence."

Aw, the reputation that follows you! The judge called both Karen and the prosecutor to chambers and questioned Karen about this allegation. Karen of course denied the allegation stating that she was fine and was just feeling under the weather a bit. The judge asked the state if they wanted a mistrial to which they said no. Karen, realizing the opportunity to have the trial ended, temporarily, would also allow her to depose the state's star witness and eventually discredit her testimony, advised the court that she would be willing to accept a mistrial and set the trial for a later date. The judge, of course, denied this request also and advised both the state and Karen that the conversation was not to leave the chambers. They did recess for the day and resumed the trial the next morning, however, not without fanfare. There on the front page of the local rag, was a complete write-up about Karen being accused of being under the influence.

Karen was infuriated, hurt and disgusted. The client also informed Karen the next day that he did not notice anything that would indicate that she had been drinking, but did think that she was exhibiting symptoms of low blood sugar, a hypoglycemic incident. He was familiar with this since his wife also had diabetes and he had witnessed her hypoglycemic effects over the years. The client stated he was satisfied with Ms. Miller's representation and it was left at that. Of course, as expected, this was not mentioned in the paper in any follow-up article.

At the conclusion of the trial the client was found guilty of manslaughter, which in a legal sense, was a win for the defense. Karen also knew that the state, and the judge, had made various tactical errors during the trial and immediately filed an appeal. Two and a half years later, the case would come back for a new trial being overturned by the Appellate Court on Karen's appeal. As I reflect now, I wish to God it never had.

In 2012, Karen decided to run for judge. Having never entertained the thought prior, and having no political experience, she decided that the only way she was going to change what was going on in the court system in our town was to become a judge. That was the one part of it. The other part was, she just didn't like the judge she planned on running against and found her condescending and arrogant. Karen also felt that this judge treated every lawyer that came before her, including Karen, with admonition and contempt, except of course, the prosecutors. This judge had been on the bench for fourteen years and to Karen, displayed an attitude that she was "entitled" to the seat, and had become very powerful, perhaps too powerful, in her position.

Karen also told me that it was no secret that she was not very well received, or liked, by some of the other judges.

We went about filing the campaign documents, campaigning, and spending all of our spare time putting up signs and standing on street corners waving to passing motorists. And of course, there was the press, which took great pleasure in bringing up Karen's past each and every time a story was written about the election. And, not out of coincidence, shortly after Karen announced her intent and filed the campaign documents, the Florida Bar got involved. Trying to run a grass roots campaign against a very powerful sitting woman judge was tough enough in and of itself, but throw in the press negativity at every chance, and now the Florida Bar making her jump through hoops, Karen was being stretched in every direction and started drinking more and more. As a result of the complaints to the Bar, Karen also lost her Board Certification, even though the two were not related. The loss of the certification came as a result of unknown "peers" giving negative reviews on Karen. Although you never know who the unknowns are, you can often surmise that it is those who have a grudge, or vendetta, against you, and both Karen and I had a good idea who they were.

She managed to hold it together for the most part, but had a period of time where she became depressed, distraught and emotionally drained. While I was asleep one night, Karen decided to get in her car and go to her office at one thirty in the morning. She was consequentially arrested for DUI, again, and it seemed like her campaign was over.

When It's Time

We decided to move forward in spite of the recent events, and Karen worked out a deal to plead Nolo Contendre, (no contest) to the 2010 DUI, which she had already done the requirements for, and the 2011 DUI was mitigated down. Of all the incidents involving Karen and her being arrested, this was truly the one that she admittedly was guilty of, and she accepted the consequences. Unfortunately, it also negated the opportunity for her to be vindicated from the arrest that led to her firing, and to show, what both she and I felt, was that the officer involved in the 2010 arrest was merely out for retribution.

Karen and I travelled to all five counties during the election process, and on the night of the election, despite all the negativity, all the vengeance displayed by the press, the obvious attempt by someone to have her discredited by the Florida Bar, and very little support from her peers, Karen Elizabeth Miller took 49.1% of the vote, gathering over 65,000 votes and taking three of the five counties that the election for judge covered. While dejected that she had not won when she was so close, Karen had finally attained a level of vindication and changed the course of the future judgeship elections in this district. Running against a sitting judge here was just not done, and Karen displayed the tenacity and the courage to do it. The respect she received from her peers was astonishing, although, admittedly too late for her election. She would be encouraged to run for judge again in 2014, and prepared to do so, against the husband of the judge she just narrowly lost to. She would not get the opportunity to do so, however, and, in all likelihood, she would have won this time.

In spite of the rigors of the campaign, the arrest and the negative press, 2011, 2012 and 2013 were probably the best years of our life. Karen moved into her own office in a quaint little building downtown, Cynthia was doing very well at being a legal assistant. Our son was attending college two hours away and doing ok, as most young people do in their first time of being unsupervised, and our daughter was enjoying her school activities and cheer-leading events. The grandkids were getting older and Missi was doing well in her career. We flew to Seattle in the summer of 2011, rented a motorcycle from the local Harley dealer and spent five days touring the San Juan Islands and the Northern Washington area. Our daughter Zoe got to spend time with Karen's dad and step mom while we did.

In 2013 we flew to Colorado with our friends, Mike and Libby, rented a Harley in Denver, and spent six days touring the Rockies and Utah, spending the last two days at the same hotel we had stayed at a few years earlier. We were, at last, having fun. We started dreaming about building our house in Tennessee and in January, 2014, Karen went on a month-to-month lease for her office thinking that this may just be the year we actually did build that dream house, complete with horses and the large garden. Zoe had entered high school but indicated to us also that she was ready to move as well. Karen and I were in love beyond what either of us could imagine. We did everything together spending most of our days with each other as much as we could, and all of our nights. Karen had cut back her office hours to four days a week, took on fewer clients, and started becoming more and more comfortable with life. She had been going to a doctor for counseling and seemed to benefit from this. Then, the inevitable happened. I say the inevitable because, as it would turn out, it was the last piece of the puzzle to what would ultimately be the picture of Karen Miller's life.

The client that had been charged with the murder from thirty years ago and was ultimately found guilty of manslaughter, had the Appeal granted and contacted Karen to try his case again. Since the most he could be tried for at this point was the manslaughter charge, and if he was found guilty, most likely receive the same sentence he was currently serving, it was worth the shot. Karen, once again, took the case, pro bono. The judge in the original case had retired, but the prosecutor that made the accusation against Karen in the first trial would be doing this trial as well. To Karen, it was yet another opportunity to get vindication and show everyone just how spiteful and mean certain people in positions of authority could be. To Karen, it was her future and past, all rolled into one. Since the state had a relatively weak case to begin with, and the star witness from the first trial was not available, Karen felt that, at the very least, she could get a lesser included charge of Aggravated Battery, or, a not guilty completely, which would mean her client, now over seventy years old, would walk out the door either way. Once again, Karen went full-bore into preparing for the trial that was to take place in February, 2014.

CHAPTER SIXTEEN - "WHEN IT'S TIME"

Christmas of 2013 was marvelous. Karen once again went out and bought tons of stuff for her present and past client's children. Financially things were well, and emotionally, it seemed, Karen was doing well. We spent the week before Christmas getting the lake house ready for the renters that had rented the house every year for the past seven years during January through April. Karen loved that house, and it was truly "her" house. She picked it out, she decorated it, she furnished it and she decided what went where and when it went there.

We had a great time at Christmas, Griffin came home, all the grandkids and Karen's mother were here, and Zoe seemed to be excited about the possibility of moving to Tennessee. She had also forged a relationship with Karen over the last year and a half, the kind a young girl should have with her mother. Since Karen was going to counseling, doing all of the ridiculous stuff the Florida Bar had imposed upon her, and looking forward to the retrial, she seemed to also be looking forward to the year 2014. Karen and I spent a quiet New Year's Eve together talking about how great 2014 was going to be. Again, we were so in love and felt so close that it was a remarkable sense of accomplishment in spite of all we, and in particular she, had been through.

Valentine's Day arrived, a day that Karen always loved. She bought baskets of chocolates and candies for the parking attendants at the courthouse parking area. She always took those guys something on every holiday. I had a special gift made for her, a camera-art photo of a giant heart in luminous colors, mostly purple, Karen's favorite, and had it framed complete with matching card. The inscription on the back of the card reads "Happy Valentine's Day, with all my heart, I love you forever." That heart and a dozen yellow roses brought a giant smile to her face as she told me how much she loved me and needed me. Then, Karen went about preparing for the retrial of the client charged now with manslaughter.

The trial began on a Wednesday, I believe, and lasted two days. Since most of the witnesses from the first trial were not being used by the state or Karen, it was pretty basic. The new judge was one that Karen had been appearing before for the past few months. While she didn't think much of his abilities, or experiences as a judge at this level; he had just come from the Juvenile Division and had not been a judge at this level for long, she felt that he at least was competent to recognize her abilities and knowledge as a litigator. She could have asked for him to recuse himself since she had recently learned that he filed an anonymous complaint against her with the Florida Bar for not appearing in one of his juvenile cases, but tried to rescind the complaint when the Bar informed him they would not accept anonymous complaints. But Karen felt that, since she had been doing cases before him for the past few months, he might have garnered a new respect for her as a proven attorney, and would, at the very least, give her the opportunity for a fair trial. Prior to the trial starting, the local press again reported on the story, complete with full history of Karen's past incidences.

Here, more than two years later, Karen Elizabeth Miller was again under the scrutiny of people who have absolutely nothing to gain other than headlines. This infuriated Karen and made her want more than ever to win against this prosecutor, and against the press. It was, as I said, her opportunity for complete vindication. Karen had already completed the paperwork to run for judge again, but held off on filing them so as not to bring any attention to the trial or to anger any of the other judges. This time, it was personal, and Karen became obsessed with winning this case.

On the final day of the trial, and just before the case went to the jury, after all the testimony had been heard and all the evidence presented, Karen texted me in somewhat of a panic. "The jury is about to get the case but the state is getting afraid and have offered my client a deal if he pleads." Not understanding what kind of a deal they could possible offer at this point I texted her back, what kind of deal are they offering and is it good for the client?" She quickly replied, "They are offering him three to four more years of incarceration if he takes the deal. He is considering it now. I don't know what to do. I really want to win this and I think that I can."

When It's Time

My reply to her was one that she often said to me when getting ready for a trial and the possibility of not winning; "At the end of the day sweetheart, you go home, it is the client's decision. How much time difference if you go forward and lose?" "He's looking at another nine years or more on the original sentence, so it's a difference of about five years" she wrote back. I didn't hear from her after that regarding the outcome. A few hours later, Karen came home, somewhat depressed. Her client, it seems, had taken the plea offer at the eleventh hour and the state got out of losing to Karen Miller. To Karen, this was devastating, but I had no idea how much at the time.

Later that evening on the local on-line edition of the rag paper was the article about the conclusion and the state granting the lesser time, complete with the full dossier of Karen Elizabeth Miller's past. At the end of each article in the on-line edition people can write comments or blog about the article. Karen became incensed that the press would resort to the under belly tactics they did and try to make the whole article about her when they should have concentrated on how she got her client a lesser sentence, again, for a murder thirty years earlier.

She wrote a blog to this effect and lambasted the press for their degenerative reporting and took a shot at the state for screwing up the first trial. Shortly after that, a person who logged in as "Anonymous" replied to Karen's blog and wrote a lengthy expose on how bad Karen was, how the state was doing her a favor and how she was "well known" in this town for being a drunk and was lucky she got what she did. If Karen wasn't fully incensed at this point, she was now.

It turned out that the individual said he worked in the courthouse as a court runner or some other insignificant position, and continued to make mean, insulting and totally false accusations about Karen, the case and the trial. Karen became so enraged she offered to meet this person at her office the next day, to go over all of the evidence that the state was afraid to let in, including multiple statements from witnesses that would have most likely exonerated her client.

She even gave this anonymous individual her personal cellphone number to call her, anytime. Of course, being as this person had no actual knowledge of the facts, and felt it was amusing to trash and hurt someone anonymously (he did identify himself later on, but name only, and I knew who it was), he of course never called her, nor ever went to her office the next day, a Saturday, where Karen was waiting. To me, this is the type of person that exemplifies ignorance, intolerance and meanness, and is the type of person that should not have a position of any kind in the legal venue. This person is pure scum, and a coward to boot.

It took about a week before Karen began to come back from being depressed and hurt, despite the many accolades that were showered upon her by other attorneys and some prosecutors that were friends of hers. They all felt that she did a great job and was once again, somewhat vindicated. But Karen didn't quite see it that way and I could tell that something was just not right, she seemed out of sorts and her emotions ran hot and cold. Then she confided in me that she had been taking medications that she shouldn't because it helped her to stabilize and maintain her attitude, but now, she didn't want to take them anymore.

I didn't ask her what kinds of drugs she was doing, nor did I want to know, the only thing I said was, "how did it get like this and what are you going to do about it? I thought everything was fine for the past year and a half." She seemed surprised that I didn't want to know but simply replied, "I need to stop and that is going to require me to go through withdrawals. I need your help." Needing my help was without saying, and giving my help was without asking. Karen knew I would be there for her, and we set about trying to get over what she was going through. I would drive her to court when she didn't feel well for the next week, wait for her, bring her back home and make her dinner. We went to an outdoor function on the motorcycle where our friend's band was playing. She seemed to once again start to be her old self, happy, smiling and enjoying our time together. I hoped that we would be able to get over this, and on Monday, March 3, 2014, Karen filed her papers to run for judge. She placed them in our mailbox as she was walking out the door to go to her office.

When It's Time

That night, however, something happened that defied all reasonable logic. Karen came home, hurting, depressed and crying. The next two days were horrific for her. She would go through bouts of depression and sleep, and then become completely manic and hysterical at the same time. She indicated that she didn't want to live anymore, and wanted to kill herself. I had removed all the guns that we had from the house, all but one.

Karen had her own gun that I had bought her a few years back to keep at her office when she worked late by herself. Karen had completed a gun safety course and had a Florida Concealed Weapons Permit as well. I tried to find the gun and Karen told me, repeatedly, that she didn't know where it was. She even convinced me that I had it last and she had not seen it in weeks. I actually started to believe this.

The morning of March 6, 2014, a Thursday, things seemed to start to quiet down and Karen appeared to be more restful. I made her breakfast, took Zoe to school and came home. Karen went to her favorite supermarket in the early afternoon where she would always go and sometimes spend hours, just wandering around and talking to all the employees that knew her. She loved to go there because, as she said "everyone is nice to me there, and they all talk to me." I made her lunch and Cynthia, her assistant came to the house. Karen had called her to come by and work on a motion that had to be filed that day. A client she had just gotten a plea for and could get out of jail that night if she got the motion filed, otherwise, he would have to spend the next day in jail and maybe the weekend.

As Karen and Cynthia sat at the computer in our family room, they laughed and joked, and drank the "green tea" I had made for them. Karen told Cynthia, I hate green tea, and I'm only drinking it because he made for us." They both laughed again and Cynthia left to go file the court documents. Karen got back in her pajamas and went back to lie down.

I remember going into the bedroom and Karen telling me her legs hurt. I began to rub her legs for her and then, while kneeling on the floor in front of her, I started to cry. I don't know why I started to cry, but I did. Karen looked at me and said, "Why are you crying?" That was all she said. She didn't seem upset, she didn't seem disturbed, and she didn't really seem anything, which brought even more tears to my eyes.

The only thing I remember saying to her was, "I can't do this without you Karen, you are my life and I love you so much. Please, don't make me do this without you."

I'm not sure Karen knew what "this" was, as I am not sure I knew either. All I know is that a fear crept over me that Karen would fall back into a dependency state and everything she had worked so hard for would come crashing down again. Somehow, I think that Karen had the same fear. Karen went back to sleep until I made her something to eat for dinner. I had taken her back to the supermarket earlier since she said she needed to get some tissues and ginger ale, and waited in the car for her. As she came out, smiling, she ran into a friend of hers, a former prosecutor who had retired, and I heard her say to him as she was getting in the truck, "just send me the information and have the guy call me tomorrow." Apparently this friend had a person that needed a good attorney and he wanted Karen to handle it. We went back home and I lay down with her in bed.

My phone rang around 6:30pm and I got up to go out on the porch to answer it. It was Chuck, a friend of ours who lived around the corner. He adored Karen and worked on her campaign with her, attending every function and forming her campaign committee to collect contributions. Karen had bought him a special pair of "Grinch" pajamas for Christmas and made him wear them to our house Christmas morning for breakfast. Just before Christmas, we asked him if he was going to put any lights on his house. He told us no so, one night, Karen, our daughter and I, went to his house, wrapped several strands of lights around his chairs on his front porch, placed the chairs in front of the doorway, plugged them in, rang the bell, and ran. He opened the door, and immediately called our names. Of course, we were hiding in the bushes but made him keep the lights which he actually did wrap around the small palm tree in his front yard. We had accomplished our mission. His wife, a retired Boston police Sergeant, lived in Boston and he lived here, an arrangement that worked well for them, so he spent a lot of time with Karen and I. In addition to loving Karen as a very close friend, he also loved the very special cheesecakes and pecan pies she always made for him.

When It's Time

Later that night while I was sitting on the porch, Karen came out, fully dressed, and asked me to take her to the supermarket yet again. I told her it was almost closed and looked at the clock; it was 9:40. Since the market closed at 10:00pm, I told her I would take her and drove her up there. I waited outside and she came out with two small bags. We went back home, Karen went into the room to change and I sat on the couch, frustrated and worried. I couldn't put my finger on my emotions, or Karen's for that matter. One moment she seemed ok, the next extremely agitated. Karen began screaming in the bedroom, at nothing in particular, and slamming the cabinet doors. I went in, asked her what she was yelling at and she looked at me confused saying, I didn't know I was screaming, I'm sorry." She had every light in the bedroom, bathroom and closet on, and then began yelling at the television and the fact that she couldn't get her pants off. I helped her get her jeans off, handed her a robe and went back out to the living room. A few minutes later she came out and asked me, "Are you coming to bed soon?" "Yes," I said, "as soon as you are ready to turn off the lights and the TV and quit yelling."

Karen didn't say anything and I sat down on the couch. I wanted to go in there then, but I also knew she was aggravated about something and thought I would give her a few minutes to calm down. I don't know how long I dozed while sitting on the couch, but at 10:30pm, March 6th, 2014, Karen Elizabeth Miller ended her life.

I heard the noise, which startled me from my dozing, and ran into the closet and found her there. Our daughter also came in and was confronted with the same horrific site. The particulars of the incident aren't necessary to be discussed here, and I, nor my daughter, will ever get them out of our memories. There is really no rhyme or reason, as hard as you try to find one, for what happened, and a beautiful person was driven to the point of giving up, rather than to continue on. There's plenty of blame to go around, but the result is the same, and the decision ultimately was hers. For Karen Elizabeth Miller, "It Was Time."

The next few hours would become a chaotic blur of police and emergency workers and not knowing the extent of what happened. Zoe immediately got on her phone to the police as I was on the phone to 911. The first person that arrived I thought was a medic. He asked me where Karen was and I pointed him to the bedroom and he told me to stay where I was. At this point, I am not sure where I was, I only know that I was hysterical and crying uncontrollably.

Soon more police and emergency personnel arrived and the neighborhood became a cluster of friends and neighbors, all wondering what had happened. Our daughter called Chuck, the "Grinch," and he immediately came running in his bare feet. She also called Karen's mom and Missi, not telling them what had happened, but simply telling them they needed to come her, "now!" It was nearly two hours later that I learned from the social advocate for the police that "Karen didn't make it."

Those words have echoed in my mind since that night, and the true meaning of them has yet to set in. Neither Zoe, nor I, were allowed to leave for several hours until the police finished their investigation and took whatever they needed from the house. We were interviewed, had our hands swabbed for gunshot residue and basically held captive for what seemed like an eternity. Somewhere around 4:00am, everyone had left, and I sat down for the first time, realizing what had just transpired. I refused to believe it and fell to my knees asking God the proverbial question; "Why?" He has yet to answer.

I remember it was around 5:00am, I was standing at the front windows of our house staring out into the night, trying to get a handle on what life was going to be like after what had just taken place. I saw a marked patrol car come by the house slowly, stop, then continue on around the circle we live on. I shut off the front lights, walked outside in the darkness and stood in the front yard. The headlights from the cruiser started to go out of our little circle neighborhood, then abruptly stopped and came back towards our house. The cruiser pulled up to the house, saw me standing there, shut off the lights and this uniformed office got out and approached me.

When It's Time

I couldn't for the life of me imagine what else he could have wanted then he said, "Do you mind if I talk to you?" I of course said I did not and he came up to me, introduced himself as Officer Mike (I left the last name out intentionally), and extended his hand to mine, offering condolences. He then stated, "Your wife was an amazing woman, and I am so sorry for your loss."

Figuring that he knew her from downtown, I asked him that question. He then said, "No, I have never met her and didn't know anything about her until tonight. I was the first person to get here and I was with her when she passed away. I don't know why, but kneeling in the closet, holding her hand and talking to her, I just felt this immediate connection to her and I had to know more about her. I went back to my office, did some research on her and found out how truly amazing she was and what a wonderful person as well."

He then went on to tell me almost everything about Karen; where she went to school, that she excelled at gymnastics and what a brilliant attorney she was. He also said, "After I left the station, I just had to know more about her. She touched me so immensely in death that I wanted to know what she was in life. I went to her office, stood in the doorway gazing into the foyer, and felt overcome with what a beautiful person she was."

I was astonished that this officer, who I had never met, and by happenstance I was standing in the yard when he came by the second time, went out of his way to talk to me and say the kind things he did. For a brief moment, I felt proud of my profession again. The next day, in a house full of people, this officer came by, on his own time, and brought two bags of food for the family. He stood and talked for a bit then excused himself. I have only talked to him a couple of times after that, but he truly was a blessing that night.

The press, for the next three days, ran story after story about Karen's passing, and every story ended, or began, with her past. One station even had the audacity to call the house requesting an interview. But in fairness, every story also proclaimed what a brilliant attorney and caring woman Karen was, it was just buried between the dirt they felt necessary to throw.

The hardest part, initially, was just starting. I had to make the arrangements for the memorial service and handle the details at the funeral home. I went to the funeral home two days later, accompanied by Missi, Pastor Danny, and Karen's mother. After settling on what was to be done, I was handed a book that contained sayings and blessings to be put on the Remembrance Cards to be handed out at the memorial. I didn't know what to put on there, but I knew that I didn't want some clichéd phony tribute that was not reflective of Karen. I scanned several pages, then, like a light, it penetrated me; I had found the perfect saying, one that epitomized Karen, and everything she stood for. I tried to read it out loud for everyone to hear and agree upon, but only got the first sentence out before I started to cry. The words that we all chose for Karen's card were from a poem by Ralph Waldo Emerson, it goes like this:

"To laugh often and much; to win the respect of intelligent people and the affection of children; to earn the appreciation of honest critics and endure the betrayal of false friends; to appreciate beauty; to find the best in others; to leave the world a bit better whether by a healthy child, a garden patch, or a redeemed social condition; to know that one life has breathed easier because you lived here, This is to have succeeded.

I don't know exactly when these words were penned by Mr. Emerson, but he truly had Karen Elizabeth Miller in mind when he put them to paper. For every line of this poem, was her.

On March 15, 2014, a Memorial Service was held for Karen at our church, and presided over by Pastor Danny. Over one thousand people attended, and the church, a large Baptist Church, was standing room only. I tried to adhere to what Karen had always said she wanted at her funeral, but I did draw the line at the Elvis impersonator. The service started with a saxophone solo by another friend; "Bridge Over Troubled Waters," and it ended with a very close friend of ours singing "Are You Lonesome Tonight," the one song Karen had always made me promise to have sung at her funeral. I never thought I would have to do it, and at the conclusion of the song, you could hear people crying uncontrollably.

When It's Time

Prior to the service, and at the conclusion, there was a video slide show of Karen's life running continuously with over one hundred photos of her, our family, our friends and our trips. In every photo, Karen displayed the beautiful smile she always had, up until the very end. And almost every photo showed Karen wearing the large gold chain with the purple stone I had set for her. While the last song was being played, a photo of Karen walking off into the woods at our property in Tennessee was shown, and, to that, I bid my darling wife farewell in this life, until we meet again.

There were two people of significance that did not attend the service. One was my former best friend and Best Man at our wedding, the prosecutor. He didn't even call or send a card or even text me to offer condolences. But then again, why would he. The other person was Karen's former best friend and boss, the one who fired her. She was specifically asked by the family not to come. We, collectively, decided that, while she didn't end Karen's life that fateful night, she certainly was involved in it leading to that, and the pain of seeing her would have been too much for us, as a family, to deal with at that time. She violated the two rules that Karen lived by; "Loyalty to your friends, and; Innocent until proven guilty."

It may have seemed to some like a harsh move, but then our decision was justified when another friend overheard two prosecutors talking at the service. One of them asked the other, "Do you think she will show up for the service?" referring of course to the former best friend of Karen's. The response, simply stated, made me finally understand that everyone knew what this person did was wrong, it was; "I don't see why she would, or should."

At the service, as I looked out over the crowd, I saw people that Karen had touched in so many ways, and I was overwhelmed by the outpour of attendance. The only thing I could offer the congregation was; "Be nice. That's what Karen always wanted, for people to just be nice."

There were lawyers, judges, friends, police officers, Court Bailiffs, and even the ladies from the deli at the supermarket that Karen often spent many hours wandering around in talking to everyone. All of these people in one way or the other had been touched by Karen, and to them, I say thank you for honoring my wife that day.

My friend Mike, who had never met Karen, came from Utah. My friend John, who had met Karen only once briefly the summer before, came from Denver. Chuck opened his house to all of these people as a place of refuge.

One thing that remains with me is that Karen used to ask me how I could stay with someone like her who was always in some crisis. As I think I previously stated, and still believe, that is what made us as strong as we were, and what solidified our love to the point that it will never die. I told Karen I would never leave or abandon her, and to that promise I will hold true.

My family is struggling and Zoe and Griffin are taking it hard, but they are taking the steps to deal with it as best as they can, knowing their mother is not ever going to be there at the important events in their lives. Fortunately for both of them, they have long lives ahead of them and will find loves of their own to fill the void. Missi is also having a hard time with the whole thing. She was very close to Karen and loved her dearly. She is also worried about her dad, knowing that I am hurting. But as I tell her, "I am going to hurt for a long time, that's the way it is and is supposed to be."

I do want to acknowledge our good friends that have gone above and beyond in their helping us deal with this. Without them, it would have been so much more difficult. But, that is what true friends are for, isn't it, to be there when you need them and when you are struggling the most? That is a lesson that would be well to be learned by many.

The weekend before Karen's death on that fateful night, we had gone on a motorcycle ride to a reunion of retired sheriff's deputies, people that I had worked with some thirty years earlier. While Karen agreed to go, she didn't seem too excited but relished the chance to go with me and meet some of my old friends. While there, Karen spent the majority of her time with me and talking to some of the old deputies she had known, but then ventured off by herself for a while. I didn't know where she had gone but knew that she liked to wander around the stables and she was interested in gathering twigs from the wooded area around the large field that held the reunion. The event was hosted by a former deputy that I knew well but had never met his wife.

When It's Time

About a week after Karen's death, I received a single twig in the mail with a yellow ribbon attached. There was no card, letter, or any other indication of who it was from, but I immediately knew it was from my friend's wife. I contacted her through the email I had and she explained to me that she had never met Karen before, saw her briefly that day when Karen came to the house to use the bathroom, and never saw her again after that. When she read about Karen's death, she knew immediately that Karen was the person that briefly stopped into her life. She felt so emotional about Karen's passing that she penned a poem, which reads:

JUST A TWIG

I found a twig on my screen porch rail a week or so ago.
I thought it odd but did not move it.....Why, I do not know.

We had a party that very day with friends of years gone by,
I knew one of them had placed it there, did not know who or why.

My daughter came from Atlanta to visit me next day.
She asked about the twig, but there wasn't much to say.

She left it there and so did I, it was just a little twig
It seemed so insignificant, it wasn't all that big.

Another week has now passed by and sad news came this way.
A troubled soul has left this Earth but is truly at peace today.

It seems this soul was at our home and stayed for just a bit
And gathered twigs throughout the day to put on our fire pit.

When I saw her picture I immediately knew I watched her come inside
I showed her where the restroom was and continued on in stride.

I wish that I had asked her name and given her my time,
But instead I missed the chance to meet a troubled soul in kind.

We'll never know if the twig she carried was left here for a reason,
Or if it was just God's way of reminding us we're here for just a season.

Just like the twig, we all are broken, and some cannot be mended.
Karen's spirit will live on, even though her life has ended.

This poem sits quietly in a frame alongside the single twig with the yellow ribbon attached next to Karen's picture on our bookshelf at home. It is another reflection of how, one person, being touched by Karen Elizabeth Miller for one moment in time, felt so much love and compassion that she was inspired to put it into poetry and forward a memento to me. This, again, was Karen.

We all, as a family, go along now, wondering, thinking, sometimes even hating, but we go along, nonetheless. It is hard to get up every day and assess how I am going to make it without her. And it is also hard to go to bed every night knowing that I have to get up the next day, without her. But, the hardest part is realizing that a person the likes of Karen Elizabeth Miller only come around once in a millennium; and it was her time and my time to be together.

CHAPTER SEVENTEEN – EPILOGUE

As I sit and write this final chapter, tears awkwardly swell in my eyes and gently fall upon the keyboard with every stroke. Some that will read this book will find it an affront to what, or who, they think they are. Others will dismiss the words on these pages as a vain attempt to elevate Karen to a level far beyond her reality or just a husband, once again, defending the indefensible. Yet others will read the words and say, Exactly!"

I didn't write this book to slander anyone, or to satisfy some inherent need to portray Karen for anything other than what she was, I wrote this book because it is a story that needed to be told. There are thousands of people like Karen out there, searching for truth, searching for love, and searching for reality, and they, and their friends and families, need to know how special they are. But to me, there was, and always will be, only one Karen Elizabeth Miller.

Karen was indeed a complex child of God who loved everyone, no matter their status or socioeconomic situation. She never met a person she was not willing to help, and often went out of her way to help, when people needed it the most. She "laughed often," loved always and was truly the most caring, compassionate and giving individual I had ever met. For those that had the opportunity to actually know her, your lives were blessed. For those that thought they knew her but didn't, you may now have insight into this wonderful person you did not have previously. The words in this book are true, I did not embellish anything, nor would I, for Karen would not have wanted that.

The last four months have been the hardest thing I, as a man, a husband, a lover and a person, have ever had to endure. I get up every day without her and I go to bed every night crying and wondering. I know that will change over time and I will carry on, as she would want. But for now, suffice it to say that, on March 6, 2014, part of me died along with Karen. My friends always call me to ask if I am "Ok." My answer is the same, "I will never be ok, I will never stop hurting, and I will never be the same. I don't know what I will be, but "ok" isn't it."

J.T, one of my best friends, and one who was very close to Karen, probably moreso than any other of my friends, and a man of great faith, has had many conversations with me about the events that unfolded. While I chose to be "angry with God," for taking my beloved wife, J.T. tried over and over to assure me that God had indeed "answered my and Karen's prayers." Believe me, these words often fell on deaf ears, and I continually thought, "If He answered our prayers in this manner, then that was a mean and horrific way to do so. What type of God does something like this?"

My prayers were that Karen would be able to overcome her problems and lead a healthy life. Her prayers, that I often heard her repeating when she cried out to God, were to give her peace from the demons she had within. While I found it difficult to accept, J.T. would often tell me, "Karen's prayers were answered that night, as were yours. He saw his child struggling, yet again, and knew that the devil was trying desperately to take her. He brought his child home." Her prayers were answered, maybe not in the manner that any of us wanted, or like, but she is with Him, and she is at peace, I assure you of that." His assurance, for whatever it was worth, was of little comfort as I continuously fought back my anger at everything, everyone, and in particular, "GOD!"

It wasn't until several weeks later that I began to accept this premise, and would actually believe that Karen was truly "at peace, and with God." The confirmation of Karen being at peace and in Heaven would come in an unorthodox manner. I remember leaving J.T.'s house after helping him do some work on it shortly after and getting into the car I heard a song I had never heard before. It was a beautiful song and when I got home I queried the song and watched the video and listened to the song over and over. The song, by Matthew West is entitled; Save a Place for Me!" Every word in it was how I felt, and the video was remarkably touching, yet very sad. However, I also started to believe that Karen truly was with God.

When It's Time

People often talk about "soul-mates" and how they are searching for theirs or have found theirs. I never liked that phrase. I have seen too many "soul-mates" disintegrate into divorce or other tragedies, and I think the phrase is greatly abused and over used. It is, in reality, an attempt to quantify one's own life by making someone else relevant to their existence. However, I do believe that if a person makes you want to be a better person, for them, and you readily accept that opportunity, and along the way, they teach you what love really is then you have found your soul-mate. And Karen Elizabeth Miller was truly mine. Karen and I became inseparable, and our souls were truly joined. Karen taught me so much about life and love and how to be a man. When she departed this life, she simply went ahead to "Save a place for me."

A few weeks back I read an article of a compilation of books written by various authors about soul mates. Of the nine things mentioned in the article to see if you truly have found your soul mate, Karen and I had all nine. The one that struck me the most, however, was that soul mates are developed through trials and tribulations, which indeed make you stronger. Love is hard, and those that endure the hardships become true soul mates. That was Karen and I.

Rickie D. Maness

CHAPTER EIGHTEEN - THE FINAL WORDS

Some that read this ending may think I am crazy, others will understand and accept. But I have to relate what has happened since Karen's death. Everything you are about to read is true, it happened!

I was sitting on my porch, staring into space one afternoon when I had what can be called a vision, but to me, it was just a daydream. I had this vision of being called "Home" and as I was led through the light, there appeared a courtroom, or better yet, a "Judgment" room. As I was being led in by a faceless entity, the door opened and Karen was sitting at the defense table as I had seen her do so many times before. She arose as I came in, addressed the bench, where our Lord sat. Karen politely approached the bench, as my "Advocate," entered a plea of guilty, and asked the Maker to judge me accordingly with mercy and grace. My plea was accepted, I was granted immunity since my sins had already been paid for, and as we were adjourned, Karen took my hand, and we left the room, together as one. She smiled at me, gave me a hug and said, "Welcome Home." The sense of peace I felt was like none other.

I have never seen an Angel in Angelic form, never had an epiphany of sorts, never talked to a deceased relative and have never had a "burning bush" event. But I was lying in bed one afternoon a few days after I had my perceived vision when I felt like someone was in there with me and a chill came over my body. I immediately felt this need to go on the computer and query "Angels," which I did. I became obsessed with reading about Angels, life after death and communicating with loved ones who had passed. Everything I read told me this was real and then, suddenly while I was reading, an advertisement popped up for a Psychic reading. I dismissed this as just an advertisement as a result of my queries; you know that "cookie" thing that all computers are embedded with. Later that day, and the next, the same advertisement popped up, over and over and something kept drawing me to curiosity.

Eventually, I said, "what the heck, I'll give it a try." Although skeptical, having never done this before, nor actually believed it, I made the call, posted my credit card and got my first "reading" as it is referred to. The voice on the other end of the phone, Alexia, was pleasant, compassionate and comforting. I had read her bio, all the testimonials and researched her history so I felt that, at the very least, she was qualified to talk to and get a sense of understanding. And, after all, what could it hurt?

The first thing I told Alexia was I was a skeptic, and quite frankly, did not know if this was even "Biblical." She assured me she understood my skepticism and that, she herself was a Christian and that there are many references in the Bible regarding Prophets and Prophecy. We continued on.

She immediately connected with Karen, as if Karen had arranged this and was waiting for me to call. She told me things that only Karen would know, said that Karen was at peace, was learning new things but was by my side every minute. To be frank, it was somewhat overwhelming and even a little frightening. She assured me that Karen was trying very hard to communicate with me but wasn't "quite good at communicating as of yet in her new peace."

The session ended with Alexia becoming emotional and to the point of tears, apologizing but saying, "I don't usually get this emotional but the love I feel between you and Karen is so intense it has just affected me greatly. Karen is fine, she is at peace, and she is waiting for you." WOW!

I pondered what Alexia had said, not knowing if my imagination had just taken over and let me hear what I so desperately wanted to hear or if what I just witnessed was, in fact, reality of life after death. The manner of Karen's death was never discussed, nor asked about, during the reading. All I know is that, for the next several days, I talked to Karen constantly, sometimes feeling her presence, sometimes wondering why I didn't.

I had to go the lake house that weekend to clean some things up. I had not been there since the renters left. After working in the yard all day, I came in, turned the stereo on, we only get one station there, and, right on cue, our wedding song started to play. I had not heard the song for months and it shook me emotionally.

When It's Time

When I returned home, I simply asked Karen, "Darling, if you're listening to me please give me something to let me know you want to talk to me. Please tell me what to do."

Later that evening, while on the computer doing some more research and reading, I received an email from the site Alexia works for offering me another reading. I deleted it and went about my business. The next day, the same email reappeared; I booked another reading.

I had two more readings with Alexia in the next ten days, each one a little more intense, and each one more specific regarding Karen. While it made me feel somewhat at peace knowing Karen was safe, watching over me, and more importantly, "waiting" for me, it was also very frustrating believing that she was there, yet I couldn't talk to her, touch her or see her. You find yourself standing in the room yelling at nothing after a while. One thing Alexia did ask me in the last reading was, "do you have a good sense of smell; Karen tells me you do."

Actually, I do, and Karen would always chide me about how I could smell flowers and other odors before anyone else could. Alexia told me "Karen will communicate with you through a smell resembling a fruit blossom or some other flower she liked." Ok, I thought to myself, I will wait patiently for that event,

Several days later, in the middle of the afternoon, when I always take a little power nap, I was hovering between the states of sleep and awake, kind of fading off. I suddenly had this incredible flowery smell, my body tingled, and I smiled. I immediately looked at the clock to see how long I had been laying down, as I often do, and the clock read 2:50. I had only been in bed for less than twenty minutes. Again, I was overwhelmed and confused at the same time, pondering if I had just dreamed this, since I had learned that dreams are somewhat formulated on the last thing you think of before going to sleep. I got back on the computer and started doing some more research on the site that Alexia was on.

There are over three hundred and fifty Psychics and Mediums on this site, and one popped up that instantly got my attention. Walter, a medium that had been doing readings for over twenty eight years had written an article about "Talking with deceased loved ones."

I read the article, read the one hundred or so testimonials and read the answers that Walter had given to people that emailed him with questions. I was astounded at the positive things I read and the compassion and authenticity of Walter's responses to all who wrote to him. I then submitted my own question, a lengthy one, about validating the previous readings that I had had and the connection with Karen. Walter sent me a reply, part of which stated:

Dear Rick,
I can never start out without saying how sad I feel reading such a happy love but sad love ending physically. Please remember, and hold close, although she is physically absent, she is there spiritually. She sounds as she was a complex (in a good way) child of God, well accomplished and very well loved by all that had the blessing to have experienced and to have known her. As she shows she places her hand on her hand written book, (?) the long story is very well described. I hope and pray that has meaning for you.

I didn't understand the "as she shows" part or the "handwritten book" part. I had started writing this book just a few days earlier, and maybe there was some connection. Immediately I also knew that I had to talk to Walter.

Walter's appointments were booked for the next week and it did not appear as if there were going to be any openings. The next day, as I was doing some more research, Walther's picture and bio popped up offering me a reading. I went to the site and, sure enough, a cancellation had been made and I booked a reading for 5:00am the next morning. I set my alarm for 4:30am and tried to sleep, full of anticipation, yet anxiousness. When the alarm went off, I almost wasn't ready.

The phone rang promptly at 5:00am; I put in my PIN number and was connected with Walter. He asked me my name and when I told him, he said, "You are the gentleman that wrote me the question. I hope that my reply regarding the handwritten book had some meaning to you." I told him it didn't immediately but that, since I had just starting writing a book "about Karen's life," it did in that sense.

When It's Time

Walter, never asking me how Karen had died, then began connecting with her and answering the questions that I had. We spoke for nearly an hour and throughout much of the reading he continued to validate that he was indeed talking to Karen.

I could go on and on about this encounter, but I will elaborate on a few specific things that Walter asked me, things that only Karen would know, and how it really solidified what I had hoped to be true; that Karen was at peace, was in Heaven, was waiting for me, and was with me every step of the way.

"Did Karen wear a large necklace with a stone on it," Walter asked. "Yes, it was my necklace that I gave her and she had a large purple stone that I had put in a setting. She wore it always and in every picture of her, she has it on, and was wearing it when she died."

He continued; "She is holding that necklace in her hands as we read to show me how much she loves you." Now, slight goose bumps started to form on my arms as he spoke. "Karen is telling me that her death was sudden, yet anticipated, does that mean anything to you?" I didn't know how to answer this since, yes, her death was sudden, and although I never thought it would happen, I had often anticipated that it would be a possibility. Karen talked about people taking their own life often and was obsessed with celebrities that did; one in particular was Kurt Cobain. She read everything there was about that man, his life, his death, and the aftermath of both.

Walter then said to me, "Karen is telling me that you have a large scare on your back, under your left shoulder blade. Keep in mind I am dyslexic so it may be the right side. It is a unique scar." Again, right on target! I do have a unique and rather large scar under my right shoulder, the result of a tumor I had removed several years ago. It has a small dent in the middle since the growth was deeply embedded when I had it removed. Another validation of something that only Karen would know.

Walter continued, "What Karen is telling me now doesn't really have much meaning to me but maybe it will to you. She says that, when she collapsed, before her body physically hit the ground, her spirit was in Heaven." WOW! Now the goose bumps started to encase my entire body and I felt that maybe Walter was actually in touch with Karen, and that feeling was solidified with this next question.

"Rick, two days ago, did something happen at 2:50?" I asked him if he meant 2:50am or 2:50pm. "She's telling me 2:50pm, did something happen at that time?

Since I knew immediately what he was talking about, and I had only told one other person about the event of the smell at 2:50pm two days before, I was absolutely sure that Walter was authentic and Karen was there.

Walter and I talked for quite some time in which he used other references for validation and ended the reading with him telling me, "Karen will be waiting for you, she envisions reaching down, taking your hand, and leading you home, and she is always by your side. Her love for you is intense, but she wants you to be patient and have a long life ahead of you. She just didn't want to hurt anyone anymore, and is telling me she no longer needs the crutch."

As I ended the call, tears flowed from my eyes in uncontrollable fashion, and I knew my beautiful wife was at peace, with our Lord and watching over me, and the rest of the family. I had one more reading with Alexia since then and she again confirmed a connection with Karen and told me, "Karen has been quite busy getting herself together and preparing for you. Please don't take this as anything is going to happen to you soon, time in our world is much different than time in hers." Alexia also asked, "Karen didn't have a good sense of direction, did she?" I replied that she didn't, reiterating Karen' difficulties in sense of direction to which Alexia said, "Karen knows you are right where she left you and that is good."

On July 7, 2014, which would have been our 13th anniversary, I had my final reading with Walter. I booked the reading knowing that this day was going to be very hard for me, and I wanted Karen to know how much I loved, and still love, her. During the reading, there were no revelations of emotions or actions brought forth. Walter did again validate that he was "in touch" with Karen and that "she knows this day will be hard for you and is by your side." I was again assured that Karen is with me, all of us, all the time, and will be there to greet me "when it's my time." Other things talked about will remain between Karen and I but, suffice it to say, I feel her presence every day. She has assured me "to remove all doubt that I am not with you."

When It's Time

"I will not have any more readings unless some bizarre event prompts me to do so. It isn't about moving on, as some people suggest that I need to do. That, at this moment seems impossible. It's more about letting Karen move on to do what she has to do and to be there when I arrive.

I spent the afternoon sitting on the bench by the river at the old historic home we got married at thirteen years ago this day. I felt her presence, heard her laughter and know that she was sitting next to me. Then, I came home and cried.

I do feel Karen's presence in everything I do and I talk to her all the time. I know she is listening, and I know that, "when it's time," she will be there to bring me home. I truly dream about being with her and completing the mission that God put us on when He brought us together fourteen years ago.

As I wrote this book, I did not intend to exonerate Karen for some of the choices she made in her life. She holds great responsibility for putting herself in certain situations and making choices that were destined for bad endings. While Karen truly loved everyone and fought life's struggles every day, often coming out on top, her attempts at living a normal life often fell short and her demons were too much to handle as she played the final card. Others that she trusted and loved added to her downfall, each playing their own part.

There is one person in particular that I later found out had been providing Karen with the medication towards the end that ultimately took control, causing her to lose control. He knows who he is and I saw him at the service. After I was certain in my own mind, I sent him a text telling him; "the only reason you are still alive is because I want you to go to bed each night knowing that you destroyed a beautiful person, you sent a loving family into eternal turmoil and you get to go to sleep each and every night knowing what a piece of shit you are." I never received a reply.

One thing that I have come to realize through all of this; I am now walking in Karen's shoes and understand more than ever how she felt for so many years and how hard it is to overcome tragedies such as these.

I have the same questions in my mind that Karen did many years ago; "What if I had called 911 the night before? What if I had called her doctor who would have placed her in the hospital, which would have virtually ended her career? What if I had tried harder to prevent what just might have been inevitable anyway? What if? What if?"

Maybe God put me in this position to finally understand what life is really about, and to finally understand what Karen went through all those years.

I am sure that these questions will haunt me for many years to come and I am equally sure that the answers will only come the day I am finally with her once again.

Karen and I were more than husband and wife; we were best friends, partners and lovers. Our intimate relationship left little to be desired. Karen also stood beside me when I failed as a man and a husband, not in the typical sense, but in the sense that I sometimes didn't live up to my part and took things too seriously, as I did many times throughout our marriage. Sometimes my anger got in the way of happiness for both of us, and she always brought me back around and made me love her even more, for that, I am thankful.

In addition to me wanting people to know what Karen Elizabeth Miller was, and more importantly, who she was, I also wrote this book to let people, especially friends and family, know exactly what "we" were. As you read this book, look back on the cover and see the smile, the rose, the necklace, all the things that identify Karen as "that" special person I was so blessed to have shared a life with, a life cut short by things out of our control, but a life filled with love, hope and compassion.

I've had friends that have called with condolences, some of them having lost their own spouse recently, and they all tell me, "I know it's hard, but you have to press on, that's what Karen would want." Honestly, that is the hardest part of all of this, the necessity to press on. As the days go by they don't get easier, in fact, they get harder. I feel lost, alone, empty and the thought of having to start my life over on a new journey is not in the least bit appealing to me. I find myself many times, throughout each day, thinking about the love lost and more importantly, "our" love lost.

When It's Time

I will continue to go through each day trying to press on, until such time as I no longer feel that I can, or I am able to do so without thinking. However, if the good Lord calls me home tomorrow, I will have a smile on my face. I have lived a good life, loved a good woman and have accomplished more than I ever expected to. For that, I am grateful. But, the thought of continuing my life without Karen by my side is the most difficult thing I have to deal with, and it is taking its toll.

Karen was not perfect, but she did love perfectly. All Karen ever wanted in return was to be loved. Now, maybe from above, she can see how much she truly was.

Karen Elizabeth Miller not only taught me how to love, but she taught me how to "love her," and gave me the privilege of doing so for fourteen years. I will miss her greatly for the rest of my life, but I also know that she is in Heaven, for after all, if Karen Elizabeth Miller isn't in Heaven, then there is something wrong with Heaven.

The constant smile!

Karen with her 1968 AMX Muscle Car

When It's Time

Karen in the Black Hills of South Dakota

Karen in the Blue Ridge Mountains

**So in love at our property in Tennessee
January, 2013**

Mother's Day, 2013

When It's Time

**Karen
1960 – 2014**

When We Meet Again, We'll Ride Together

Rickie D. Maness

When It's Time

Starry Night Publishing

Everyone has a story...

Don't spend your life trying to get published! Don't tolerate rejection! Don't do all the work and allow the publishing companies reap the rewards!

Millions of independent authors like you, are making money, publishing their stories now. Our technological know-how will take the headaches out of getting published. Let "Starry Night Publishing dot Com" take care of the hard parts, so you can focus on writing. You simply send us your Word document and we do the rest. It really is that simple!

The big companies want to publish only "celebrity authors," not the average book-writer. It's almost impossible for first-time authors to get published today. This has led many authors to go the self-publishing route. Until recently, this was considered "vanity-publishing." You spent large sums of your money, to get twenty copies of your book, to give to relatives at Christmas, just so you could see your name on the cover. Now, however, the self-publishing industry allows authors to get published in a timely fashion, retain the rights to your work, keeping up to seventy-percent of your royalties, instead of the traditional ten-percent.

We've opened up the gates, allowing you inside the world of publishing. While others charge you as much as ten-thousand dollars for a publishing package, we charge less than three-hundred dollars to cover proofreading, copyright, ISBN, and distribution costs. Do you really want to spend all your time formatting, converting, designing a cover, and then promoting your book, because no one else will?

Our editors are professionals, able to create a top-notch book that you will be proud of. Becoming a published author is supposed to be fun, not a hassle.

At Starry Night Publishing, you submit your work, we proofread it, create a professional-looking cover, a table of contents, compile your text and images into the appropriate format, convert your files for eReaders, take care of copyright information, assign an ISBN, allow you to keep one-hundred-percent of your rights, distribute your story worldwide on Amazon, Barnes & Noble and many other retailers, and write you a check for your royalties. There are no other hidden fees involved! You don't pay extra for a cover, or proofreading. You will never pay to keep your book in print. We promise! Everything is included! You even get a free copy of your book and unlimited discount copies.

In twelve short months, we've published more than three-hundred books, compared to the major publishing houses which only add an average of six new titles per year. We will publish your fiction, or non-fiction books about anything, and look forward to reading your stories and sharing them with the world.

We sincerely hope that you will join the growing Starry Night Publishing family, become a published author and gain the world-wide exposure that you deserve. You deserve to succeed. Success comes to those who make opportunities happen, not those who wait for opportunities to happen. You just have to try. Thanks for joining us on our journey.

www.starrynightpublishing.com

www.facebook.com/starrynightpublishing/

Made in the USA
Charleston, SC
16 May 2015